T0319035

Cambridge Elements ⯘

Elements in Public and Nonprofit Administration
edited by
Andrew Whitford
University of Georgia
Robert Christensen
Brigham Young University

APPLES TO APPLES

A Taxonomy of Networks in Public Management and Policy

Branda Nowell
North Carolina State University

H. Brinton Milward
University of Arizona

CAMBRIDGE
UNIVERSITY PRESS

University Printing House, Cambridge CB2 8BS, United Kingdom

One Liberty Plaza, 20th Floor, New York, NY 10006, USA

477 Williamstown Road, Port Melbourne, VIC 3207, Australia

314–321, 3rd Floor, Plot 3, Splendor Forum, Jasola District Centre,
New Delhi – 110025, India

103 Penang Road, #05–06/07, Visioncrest Commercial, Singapore 238467

Cambridge University Press is part of the University of Cambridge.

It furthers the University's mission by disseminating knowledge in the pursuit of
education,learning, and research at the highest international levels of excellence.

www.cambridge.org
Information on this title: www.cambridge.org/9781108987462
DOI: 10.1017/9781108987646

First published 2022

A catalogue record for this publication is available from the British Library.

ISBN 978-1-108-98746-2 Paperback
ISSN 2515-4303 (online)
ISSN 2515-429X (print)

Apples to Apples

A Taxonomy of Networks in Public Management and Policy

Elements in Public and Nonprofit Administration

DOI: 10.1017/9781108987646
First published online: June 2022

Branda Nowell
North Carolina State University

H. Brinton Milward
University of Arizona

Author for correspondence: Branda Nowell, branda_nowell@ncsu.edu

Abstract: Interest in networks in the fields of public management and policy has grown to encompass a wide array of phenomena. However, we lack a stable and empirically verifiable taxonomy for delineating one network class from another. The authors propose all networks and multi-organizational collaborative entities can be sorted into three taxonomic classes: structural-oriented, system-oriented, and purpose-oriented. This Element reviews the intellectual disciplinary histories that have informed our understanding of each of the three classes of networks. It then offers a taxonomic description of each of these networks. Finally, it provides a field guide for empirically classifying networks. The authors hope the taxonomy presented will serve as a tool to allow the field to quicken the pace of learning both within and across classes. When we are able to compare apples to apples and avoid inadvertent comparison of apples and oranges, we all get smarter faster.

Keywords: networks, partnerships, collaboration, collaborative governance, network management

ISBNs: 9781108987462 (PB), 9781108987646 (OC)
ISSNs: 2515-4303 (online), 2515-429X (print)

Contents

1 Why Do We Need a Taxonomy in the Study of Networks?

Scholars of the social world are dedicated to the study of the intangible. We give names to things, we create conceptual boundaries in an effort to distinguish these things from other things, and collectively, we attempt to build a body of knowledge about something that has neither weight nor mass. Periodically, it is useful for a field to reflect on this practice. In 1897, Spencer challenged the nascent field of sociology to grapple with whether "society" could be regarded as an entity, distinguishable from other social entities. In this Element, we tackle the same challenge as we attempt to answer this question about the burgeoning literature on networks in the fields of public management and policy.

Networks in Public Management and Policy Studies

The study of networks of public and nonprofit organizations entered the lexicon in the late 1980s and early 1990s. Since that time, a once small community of network scholars has grown into a large, vibrant, and heterodox community. The study of networks in the field of public management and policy has expanded rapidly to encompass a wide array of contexts and phenomena. Among scholars contributing to this growing literature, there seems to be an implicit belief that not all networks are created equal; that "network type" matters in the application of relevant theory as well as the generalizability of results (Brown & Keast, 2003; Keast et al., 2004; Rethmeyer & Hatmaker, 2008; Isett et al., 2011; Kapucu et al., 2014; Lecy et al., 2014). As a result, scholars have sought to differentiate, categorize, and characterize network phenomena using a number of different labels. For example, it might seem reasonable to assume that the theoretical mechanisms and dynamics in contexts labeled as "governance network" will be similar to each other and characteristically different from a context labeled "goal directed network," or "service delivery network." However, most of these characterizations have neither a stable definition of attributes nor a robust theory to illuminate their implications relative to networks that do not conform to these attributes.

We argue the challenge is not the diversity of the phenomenon loosely coupled via a network perspective, nor is the problem the diversity of perspectives brought to bear in explaining networks operating in the public sphere. On the contrary, this diversity is a considerable strength and opportunity in the field. **What is a limiting factor is the lack of a taxonomy allowing scholars to communicate with each other, not to mention with students and policymakers, about this diversity in a manner that allows for the comparison of apples to apples.** This Element is an attempt to classify public management and policy network research into a taxonomy that organizes the many different network types in use today and differentiates one type from another in a way that allows for the advancement of both theory and practice. Our interest is in classifying variation in the existential nature of the network entities studied in public management and policy and in providing scholars with an empirically verifiable set of delineating characteristics to guide this classification effort.

Proliferation of Network Labels: Defining the Problem

The concept of "a network" has had broad appeal, in part, because it has such intuitive flexibility. Once you start thinking about networks, you will likely not be able to stop yourself from seeing them everywhere. You will see them when you go to the grocery store and think about how your avocado made it from an organic farm in California to a grocery store in North Carolina. You will see them in your workplace in the patterns of alliances that you observe among your colleagues and among departments. You will see them in a morning news story of newly discovered terrorist cells found to be connected to a recent bombing in Syria. You will see them at your child's school as you struggle getting all the different specialists on the same page in developing a coherent plan for your child, who has special healthcare needs. You will see them at the organizing meeting you attend as a volunteer for an environmental group that is trying to address climate change.

The flexibility and broad applicability of network concepts and theories is particularly evident in the range of social contexts represented in scholarship about networks in public management and policy. By context, we are referring specifically to the actual entity being labeled as "a network" – not in the abstract, not metaphorically, but in specific instances. Coupled with this diversity of contexts is a sizable array of lenses and associated labels that scholars use to understand networks. These lenses are anchored in competing root metaphors as well the disciplinary agendas of various network scholars that we will discuss in subsequent sections. Again, neither this diversity of contexts nor the diversity of lenses within which to understand them constitutes a problem. In fact, we see this as a major strength of the field.

The problem is that **we have no taxonomy with which to describe and differentiate different classes of networks outside of the lens we are using to understand it**. This has led to a proliferation of labels delineating "network types," which conflate the lens used to understand the network with the network itself. The field of public management and policy has spawned a plethora of labels for collaborative phenomena. The landscape is littered with labels like interorganizational networks, policy coalitions, whole networks, public management networks, governance networks, policy subsystems, cooperative networks, coordinative networks, policy formation networks, mixed form governance networks, community coalitions, public–private partnerships, disaster response or emergency management networks, goal-directed networks, cross-sector collaborations, policy implementation networks, collaborative governance regimes (CGRs), and policy networks. Some will remember the 1988 British comedy with Michael Palin (formerly of Monty Python), Jamie Lee Curtis, and Kevin Kline in *A Fish Called Wanda*. It was a wonderful caper movie that featured a much-loved goldfish named Wanda. Many network scholars have their Wanda's. Milward and Provan (2006) have four. Each different from the other based on a label, limited specification, a general description, and an example.

- Information Diffusion Networks: The Global Futures Forum (GFF) is a multinational community limited to governmental intelligence organizations and other governmental organizations focused on foreign, internal, or international security issues that work at the unclassified level to make sense of emerging and future transnational and global security challenges (Wikileaks, 2011).
- Problem-Solving Networks: A Wildfire Incident Command System deals with a predicable problem like wildfires or floods that occur at regular intervals (Moynihan, 2009).
- Community Capacity-Building Networks: The Drug and Alcohol Recover and Education (DARE) network that used cops to teach kids about the dangers of drug use so they would be more likely to resist peer pressure to use them. This network persisted for many years despite mounting evidence that it was ineffective (Frumkin & Reingold (2004).
- Service Implementation Networks: These networks consist of contracts that link a set of service providers to a network administrative organization that acts to govern the network. In economic terms, the network has a joint-production function (Provan & Milward, 1995).

While all four types of interorganizational networks in the Milward and Provan (2006) typology have intuitive appeal such that scholars can put a name with a network, they are by no means unique or mutually exclusive. Each type merely reflects a different function that a network can exhibit, and it is possible to imagine one network that combines all of these functions. A healthcare network could be a service implementation network that links providers to clients. In a pandemic like COVID, it may be called upon to mount a mass vaccination campaign. To encourage vaccination, it may need to diffuse information about the safety and efficacy of the vaccines. In preparing to manage ongoing and future infectious diseases, it will need to work with its network of providers to build community capacity to better withstand the next public health crisis. Types based on function are illustrative but do not serve to tell us that this network is different or similar in theoretically significant ways relative to other networks.

Other typologies that have sought to offer some organization to the plethora of ambiguously interrelated labels include early typologies by Brown, Keast, Mandell, and colleagues (Brown & Keast, 2003; Keast et al., 2004) who argued networks could be usefully categorized into three types: cooperative, coordinative, and collaborative. However, as pointed out by subsequent scholars (e.g., Lecy et al., 2014), delineation of these types focuses on the nature of interactive processes present and necessary capabilities for enacting these processes. While useful as a diagnostic and for advancing process theories in collective efforts, it is limited in helping us to distinguish one entity from another, as it was hard to imagine a network that only did one of these things at the exclusion of all others.

Similarly, review articles by Isett et al. (2011) and Kapucu et al. (2014) described three main types of networks: collaborative networks, policy networks, and governance networks. The distinguishing feature here being networks that respectively are all policy action (policy networks), all improvement of public good, service or value (collaborative networks), or a mix of the two (governance networks). Like the network named Wanda, this is also a useful heuristic, but in reality, it is unclear how many networks exist in the world that constrains their activities in this way. Based on existing studies there is reason to believe they may be quite rare. There is ample scholarship to suggest that improving public goods/public value often requires policy changes (Foster-Fishman et al., 2007; Pollack Porter et al., 2018) and it is hard to envision many public policy agendas that are not tied in some way to improving public goods or public value. We have yet to see scholarship employing this classification scheme justify its use through any sort of empirical confirmation that the network in question does only one of these activities to the exclusion of the others. Further, even if such delineations were reflective of practice, the theoretical relevance of these qualities is as yet underdeveloped. For example, are the collaborative processes, structures, and capabilities for changing policy through networks fundamentally distinct from the processes, structures, and capabilities needed for improving a public good through networks? Perhaps. However, this seems more reasonable as an empirical question rather than a taken-for-granted assumption that divides a literature.

We Need a New Direction

Our intent is not to litigate the conceptual distinctiveness of the myriad of labels associated with network entities; that ship has sailed. We are not interested in wading into debates about whether governance networks are different from (Kapucu & Hu, 2020), the same as (e.g., Klijn, 2020), subordinate to (e.g., Kenis, 2016), or superordinate of (e.g., Koliba et al., 2018) collaborative networks. It is our belief that the use of these labels generally offers far more insight into the disciplinary background and research agenda of the author than provides clarity about the delineating characteristics of the entity of interest. Most commonly, scholars (ourselves included) employ a conceptual lens and research interest, say in policy making or collaborative service delivery *through* networks, and subsequently label our focal network in accordance with this interest.

In this way, these labels are failing us. We cannot continue to confuse the entity, itself, with the lens used to understand it. Why? Because we assert there are real, meaningful, and theoretically important differences in the variety of entities labeled as "networks" in the field of public management and policy. Creating a taxonomy of entities that allows for the classification of networks as either unlike or like other entities is an important step forward for a scientific field. This is not a plea for scholars to stop using their preferred labels; rather, **it is a plea for scholars to provide specific information about the delineating characteristics of their entity of interest in conjunction with those labels so we can all get smarter faster.** If we are to advance theories unique to these specific entities, we need to be able to distinguish scholarship and theorizing situated within one network entity from theories and research situated within another. A taxonomy should identify network classes based on clear criteria that can be applied to delineate entities that fundamentally differ from one another in theoretically important ways, and therefore can be presumed to be relatively incomparable. This does not mean that concepts relevant to one class cannot have relevance for another class; only that translation of concepts and theories across classes must be done with careful attention to what makes the classes unique. To abuse our title-track apples metaphor, we need to be able to distinguish scholarship on the apple networks from the scholarship on the orange networks. Equally important, if we are to leverage the interdisciplinary advantages of our field, scholars examining the same network from the perspective of different lenses need to be able to talk to each other (Lemaire et al., 2019). If we are all studying apples but calling them different things, our progress in understanding apples will be slow at best.

Need for a Taxonomy

In the *Architecture of Complexity*, Herbert Simon (1962) argued that hierarchical systems will evolve more rapidly than nonhierarchical systems because subsystems create stable entities that can be put together to form more complex entities. It is for this reason that disciplines form from aligned subdisciplines comprised of compatible domains of inquiry. While there are downsides to this – requiring fields to be mindful of integration as well as differentiation to avoid ideas clustering into impermeable silos – differentiation is both important and inevitable as complexity increases (Simon, 1946; Lawrence & Lorsch, 1967). Applied in the context of research areas such as the study of networks, taxonomic definitions and categories create the basis for assigning different theoretical mechanisms to different network types, creating a shorthand, such that a network occupying a certain taxonomic category can be assumed to be consistent with the features unique to that category. When the taxonomy is applied correctly, this creates a measure of control for those features within the various types of networks, allowing scholars to better focus on the variables of interest believed to vary within that type. Without a robust taxonomy, the applicability of findings from one network study to another is at best unclear, at worst inappropriate. **The central argument of this Element is that scholarship on networks in public management and policy lacks a theoretically robust taxonomy for meaningfully characterizing and categorizing networks and related phenomen**a; in fact, it lacks any taxonomy.

What Is a Taxonomy?

Smith (2002) argues there are two basic approaches to classification. The first is typology, which conceptually separates a given set of items multi-dimensionally. The key characteristic of a typology is that its dimensions represent *concepts* rather than empirical *cases*. The dimensions are based on the notion of an ideal type, a mental construct that deliberately accentuates certain characteristics, not necessarily something found in empirical reality (Weber, 1949). As such, typologies create useful heuristics and provide a systematic basis for comparison. Their central drawbacks are categories that are neither exhaustive nor mutually exclusive, are often based on arbitrary or ad hoc criteria, are descriptive rather than explanatory or predictive, and are frequently subject to the problem of reification (Bailey, 1994).

A second approach to classification is taxonomy. Taxonomies differ from typologies in that they classify items based on empirically observable and measurable characteristics (Bailey, 1994, p. 6).

While taxonomies and typologies are both classification structures, the difference lies in the way in which each is developed: empirically (taxonomy) versus conceptually (typology).

A Network Taxonomy

When scholars refer to something as a "network," they should be able to clarify what they mean. A taxonomic definition does not have to be extensive to be clear. "Taxonomic definitions identify the minimum number of properties that are sufficient to demarcate one group of entities from all other entities. Their role is to demarcate the kind of entity to which a label refers, not to express in detail the nature of that kind" (Hodgson, 2019, p. 208). A taxonomic definition that is both parsimonious and clear is the one for mammals. "A mammal is a clade (branch) of animal where the females suckle their young" (Hodgson, 2019, pp. 207–208). While there are many things this definition does not tell us about mammals, there is no danger of confusing a mammal with a reptile. The usefulness of creating these definitions ensures that one person studying a class of network is talking about the same thing as someone else who is studying the same class of network. It should be noted that **it is not the task of a taxonomy to explain why networks work the way they do.**

We start this journey by asserting that **definitional to networks** *of any class* **are three core conditions:** (1) networks are fundamentally rooted in a relational perspective that considers actors and the nature of their relationships to each other, (2) networks involve at least three actors, and (3) each actor in the network is empowered with a nontrivial degree of agency or autonomy. If the first condition is not true, there is no network to consider. If the second is not true, it is purely a dyadic relation, and network perspectives and theories are likely to have limited relevance. If the third condition is not true, it is a purely hierarchical relationship between actors. While hierarchy is frequently embedded within networks (Koliba et al., 2018; Steelman, Nowell, Velez, and Scott, 2021), most network theories and concepts hinge on the assumption of horizontal interactions between actors who have some degree of autonomy. If relationships are primarily governed through hierarchy, it implies a context better fit to bureaucratic theory rather than network theories and concepts.

Three Taxonomic Classes of Networks

In light of the aforementioned three conditions, we argue the level classification of greatest theoretical import is rooted in the boundaries that delineate the entity being referred to as a network. If we can do this, we can begin to distinguish one network class from another. We focus on the definitional boundaries that constitute networks for three reasons. First, they are empirically verifiable. In order to consider a network of any type, the entity must first be recognized and legitimated as an entity and distinguished from that which is not the network. The qualities that make a network an entity can be subjected to scrutiny, verified, or challenged by outside observers. Second, the theoretical mechanisms at play under different boundary assumptions are distinct. Concepts and theories developed under one taxonomic class are not likely to transfer to another class without modification. Third, these classes offer theoretically important information about the nature of the network context itself, independent of the lens used to study it, thereby facilitating the comparison of apples to apples.

The taxonomy we propose for all networks conceptualized and studied in public management and policy can be sorted into three taxonomic classes: structural-oriented, system-oriented, and purpose-oriented. Each class has a different theoretical base: structural-oriented networks view the world from a relational perspective with a focus on understanding network effects on individuals and ties; system-oriented networks are theoretically anchored in systems, policy domains, and policy subsystems' perspectives; purpose-oriented networks are theoretically anchored in the social psychological literature on the formation of groups and collective action within organized collectives.

The following are the taxonomic definitions of each class of networks.

Structural-Oriented Networks

Taxonomic Definition: Structural-oriented networks are representations of social structure with arbitrary analyst-imposed boundaries; **these networks are delineated from the other classes in that the collection of actors and their ties are not presumed to represent any higher-order entity**.

Scholars create structural-oriented networks by applying graph analytic techniques (i.e., social network analysis) to a sample population of nodes to understand the consequences of social structure for either nodes or ties. Structural-**oriented studies of networks are either egocentric or dyadic in nature.** The delineation between these two subtypes is whether the theoretical focus is on the node or edge (or both). Nodes refer to actors within a network that have agency to make or delete ties. Edges refer to ties between actors on some predefined relationship (e.g., friendship, communication, advice giving). In **dyadic** studies, networks are conceptualized and delineated in terms of aggregates of their most fundamental unit of measure – the characteristics of a relationship of one actor to another actor in a population of interest. Key questions within this class of research focus on explaining variation in partner selection (who interacts with whom and why) and the quality and nature of ties (e.g., for review, see Sicilliano et al., 2021. Studies of patterns of diffusion of innovation through networks are a common example of this type of network research (e.g., Damanpour, 1991).

The second type of structural-oriented networks is ego networks. In this type, networks are conceived of as attributes of actors, often viewed as strategic assets that can be manipulated and organized by the actor in pursuit of their objectives. Burt's (1995) structural hole theory is a modern and methodologically sophisticated example. It can explain managers' promotions (Burt, 1995), their creativity (Burt, 2004), and the formation of interlocking directorates (Burt, 1995). This kind of theory is advanced by demonstrating its broad applicability, its scope conditions, and contingencies (Burt, 1997). These networks can also be viewed as a source of constraint for an actor, reinforcing specific norms, values, and ideas and serving to create a redundancy of information exchange (e.g., Coleman, 1988; Burt, 2001). Egocentric and dyadic structural-oriented networks are discussed in depth in Section 3.

System-Oriented Networks

Taxonomic Definition: System-oriented networks are networks for which **the network and its boundaries are a reflection of analyst-imposed decision rules presumed to delineate the relevant population of actors, and their relations, associated with some system of interest**.

Systems of interest generally refer to a system for managing some issue of public concern or public policy. For example, systems for managing watersheds, responding to domestic violence, reducing teen pregnancy, or delivering health care to a given population of individuals are all systems of interest for which system-oriented network studies have been conducted. These networks are defined and literally brought into being by a network analyst – the person who conceives of the network – and do not have an agreed-upon identity outside of the imaginings of the analyst. The network analyst may be a scholar, policy maker, or practitioner. Laumann et al. (1983) referred to these networks as nominalist networks, stating that "Here, the analyst self-consciously imposes a conceptual framework [of the network] constructed to serve his or her own analytic purposes" (p. 66). The network analyst does this by way of applying implicit or explicit decision rules that define who is and is not relevant to the system of interest and subsequently, to the network. As such, issues of boundary specification within the use and study of system-oriented networks are particularly paramount as different analysts, policy makers, or practitioners may look at the same system and yet conceive of the relevant network of actors quite differently (Nowell et al., 2018). Issues of boundary specification in system-oriented networks are discussed in Section 4.

Purpose-Oriented Networks

Taxonomic Definition: Purpose-oriented networks are networks that have self-actualized as entities by meeting the criteria of **being bounded, self-referencing collectives comprised of actors who consciously affiliate to the collective around some shared purpose**. A network is bounded when members can reliably identify other members and distinguish them from nonmembers. A network is self-referencing when it gives itself a name and gains a collective identity as an entity associated with its stated purpose.

While each actor in a purpose-oriented network will have their own portfolio of unique interests, ambitions, and motivations for affiliating with the collective, there is some common sense or recognition of a shared purpose for why the collective exists. As such, the purpose-oriented network is **sociologically real** to its members. By this, we mean that **purpose-oriented networks have established a shared identity, and members both endorse their affiliation with this shared identity** and **have a means by which they can reliably identify other members and distinguish them from nonmembers.** This shared identity is generally based around some articulation of a concern. Burns and Stalker (1961) described "a concern" as the focus around which purposeful organizing occurs. In order for an organization to exist, there must be a shared concern or purpose around which organizing occurs. In the same way, in order for a network to be self-referencing, a concern must also exist as this concern or purpose is the reason for both affiliation and organizing. Further, members must have instituted some type of forum for convening members around the concern.[1] Examples of these kinds of networks include a Firewise Council comprised of public and private landowners and other stakeholders who meet regularly to identify actions to improve wildfire resilience of their community or a community collaborative comprised of representatives of organizations and agencies who serve the homeless population who meet regularly to share information and identify service gaps and redundancies.

In the following sections, we present this taxonomy in detail and apply it as an organizing framework to help bring greater clarity and definition to the current literature of networks in public management and policy. In Section 2, we begin by tracking the intellectual lineages that have shaped the current approaches and agendas that define the study of networks within the field. We examine the disciplinary lenses that have come to inform our different assumptions and approaches in studying networks. In Sections 3–5, we take a deeper look at each of these three classes of networks with a focus on the network literatures most

---

[1] For additional discussion on purpose-oriented networks, see Carboni et al., 2019

aligned with each class. Finally, in Section 6, we focus on analysis and integration, offering tools and frameworks for positioning network studies within the appropriate class and considering points of intersection across classes.

Scope of Our Taxonomy

Taxonomic categories of social phenomena are human-created categories, not biophysical phenomena. Our taxonomy is anchored in empirically verifiable characteristics to aid in classification. In Section 6, we present empirical validation metrics for determining network class. **Each class is mutually exclusive based on its delineating characteristics but an analyst may hold an interest in multiple classes of networks within the same context simultaneously.** For example, an analyst may identify one or more purpose-oriented networks as relevant to a broader system-oriented network of interest. However, the nature of the networks themselves remain conceptually distinct and networks of different classes studied in the same setting should not be confused. The delineating characteristics for each class are intended to be both theoretically meaningful – but perhaps even more important – empirically verifiable. Thus, they are both derived and observed.

System-oriented and purpose-oriented networks seem to fit neatly into the public management and policy portfolio as there are many examples in the literature. There are fewer examples of structure-oriented networks. Perhaps this is because network analysis in our field is a mix of organizational and institutional analysis with a bit of social network analysis thrown in. The reason for keeping structure-oriented networks as a distinct class is that this is where the study of networks began in sociology and anthropology and where methods for analyzing social networks developed.

Limitations and Reasonable Debates

There are three major points where we see an emerging debate among scholars of public management and policy scholars over our taxonomy. This is perfectly reasonable and likely to improve research in our field. The first is concern over the preservation of existing labels. Scholars will continue to use various labels for networks. It is hard to not name something based on one's scholarly focus, like service implementation. This is not inappropriate and may lead to clarification about processes and structures that facilitate a given function of interest so long as we are cautious to not conflate the function an entity performs with the entity itself. A second point of debate is our classification of entities within the literature where the originating authors have elected to use labels that do not include the term "network" in referring to these entities. A third critique is rooted in the argument that networks are a phenomenon best studied by social network methods and if collaborative phenomena are not studied that way, they are some other type of social object.

Regarding the first point, public management and policy scholars (ourselves included) have created a plethora of names for networks. As we discuss later in this Element, many of these network labels generally fall within one class. However, it is not uncommon for different authors to apply the same label to networks fitting in different network classes. Hence, the need for the taxonomy to avoid confusion. An interesting alternative to our taxonomic approach has been advocacy by some who study a given class of networks to reserve the term "network" to refer solely to one class to the exclusion of the others. For example, we have heard from those who use the term "network" to refer to purpose-oriented networks insist that system-oriented networks are not really networks, they are systems within which networks organize. At the same time, we have heard those who study system-oriented networks insist that purpose-oriented networks are not networks at all but rather forums within larger networks. We find this discussion entirely circular and counterproductive for the field. The fact of the matter is that the term "network" is extensively used in the literature to refer to a variety of phenomena that span these three classes. In our view, we are long past the point of any one camp claiming exclusive ownership of the term "network." What is needed, in our opinion, is an empirically verifiable classification so that literature concerning phenomena of the same class can be meaningfully compared and avoid unwitting comparison of entities of different classes.

We do not expect that our taxonomy will supplant the many network labels that already exist; however, it is our hope that taxonomic class will eventually become part of the definition used to describe networks. Because different scholars may apply labels differently, network labels should not presume a given network class unless the community of scholars invested in that label makes the network class explicitly definitional to the subtype. Fitting a particular network into its correct taxonomic class is the task of the network analyst and the peer-review process. The goal of this Element and the accompanying taxonomy is to bring a degree of order to an orchard where everybody seems to want to plant a different fruit tree. We seek to offer a common framework that will allow for greater appreciation across scholars of the diversity of scholarship aimed at understanding networks in public management and policy arenas. In this spirit, our last section (i.e., Section 6) is, "The Pocket Field Guide to Classifying Networks."

A second debate surrounding this taxonomy is whether it is reasonable and productive to apply our taxonomy to classify scholarship where the originating author does not embrace the term "network" but still refers to an entity that consists of three or more relatively autonomous actors that have some relationship to one another that is not purely hierarchical. Examples include references in the literature to partnerships, coalitions, and CGRs. A core premise of this Element is that the literature is hindered by the expansion of different labels that refer to similar phenomena. In the following sections, we map the definitions, origins, and illustrative examples of the entities bearing these labels against our taxonomy. We assert that, based on our taxonomic definition, there is theoretical reason to believe these entities are meaningfully related to literatures that refer to, for example, goal-directed networks and whole networks also fitting this class. Regardless of how we refer to these entities, we see this as an opportunity for allowing these literatures to co-inform one another. Again, our intent is not to direct who should or should not use what labels. Rather, we seek to provide an empirical basis for comparison of phenomena of a similar class, and differentiation from other classes, regardless of the label used.

Last, we have heard advocacy by scholars who are resistant to the notion of networks being subdivided into classes and prefer to conceptualize "networks" as a unidimensional concept that takes different forms depending on your level of analysis. This is a tradition that is rooted in social network analysis, rather than in classification of distinctive sociological phenomenon. In advocating for this position, the tendency is to focus on what our three classes hold in common – for example, all three classes can be studied using social network methods and models; the study of all three require careful attention to the analytical decisions made; all three classes can be investigated using data situated at individual, dyadic, cluster, or network levels. We agree with all these points in terms of what all three network classes hold in common. However, the existence of commonalities across classes does not negate the existence of theoretically meaningful classes. Amphibians and mammals also have commonalities. Our intent in this Element is not to focus on commonalities across classes but rather explicate root characteristics that delineate three network classes that differ from each other in fundamentally important ways such that theoretical comparisons across classes should be done with care and attention to what makes these classes unique.

In our taxonomy, what defines the network class is not the method used to understand a network nor the level of analysis one embraces. Rather, network class is determined based on the existential nature of the entity of interest and the extent to which the attributes of that entity correspond to the delineating characteristics of the class (see discussion in subsection "Unit of Theory" in classifying networks). Specifically, class is determined by whether the network phenomena is (a) a self-actualized entity based on the three criteria of self-reference, bounded membership, and conscious affiliation around a shared purpose, (b) a non-self-actualized set of actors and their relationships identified based on a set of analyst-imposed decisions rules deemed to represent a system of interest, or (c) an emergent social structure based on an analyst imposed sampling frame intended to represent *neither* a self-actualized entity nor a broader system of interest. In other words, what we are interested in classifying in this Element is variation in the existential nature of the network entity of interest. This, in our view, is key to making progress in understanding the role that networks play in public administration and in implementing public policy.

Final Note: Network as Verb versus Noun

The concept of a network is powerful in part because it sits at the intersection of process and structure. At their core, networks of any class are the manifestations of intentional efforts by actors to create connection and engage in activity that is embedded within, shaped, and constrained by connectivity with others. In this way, there is an argument to be made that network is best understood as a verb, a dynamic action or set of actions that collectively culminate into higher-order phenomena that are simultaneously emergent and deterministic (Berthod & Segato, 2019). This approach to viewing networks as processes rather than entities is consistent with early organizational theorists such as Karl Weick (1989) who urged the field to view organization not as a noun, but as a verb, organizing reflecting a pattern of communication and coordinated set of actions, similar to jazz improvisation. Similarly, Feldman and Sengupta (2020) have argued for the value of process theories for advancing a logic of possibility as opposed to probability in understanding organizational behavior.

We wholeheartedly agree that there is much to be gained from process theories of networks and networking; from viewing network as a verb, not a noun. It has always seemed odd to us that structural perspectives on networks (networks as nouns) and process perspectives on networks (network as verb) are often viewed as competing rather than complementary perspectives. We disagree with this entirely. In our view, structure and process are entirely co-determinant. Structure emerges from process and yet, as processes of structuration advance, a relatively stable structure emerges (Giddens, 1984). These structures create the context that subsequently serves to shape and constrain further processes. In other words, structure is created through process and yet at the same time, process always occurs within structure. To understand one, it is important to understand the other.

What does this have to do with a network taxonomy? Our network taxonomy seeks to organize efforts focused on viewing networks as entities (i.e., nouns) – viewed as such either by the analyst or by the network members themselves.

While the role of process theory within this taxonomy is outside the scope of this Element, it is our hope that this taxonomy will help to serve as a point of integration for positioning process theories within the appropriate network class. We view this taxonomy as a framework that can aid scholars to consider the context within which different processes of organizing, be it collaboration, coordination, or simply communication (e.g., Keast et al., 2007) are occurring.

2 The Intellectual Development of Three Disciplinary Lenses on Networks

In this section, we consider three disciplinary lenses that we argue have had a strong influence in shaping the study of networks in public management and policy. As shown in Figure 1, these lenses have considerable intellectual overlap and yet they reflect distinct traditions and histories. We have labeled these lenses organizational, policy, and community planning.

The Evolution of the Organizational Lens on Networks

The organizational lens on networks emerged out of research in the 1960s that challenged classical and neoclassical notions of organizations as closed systems. During this period, there was heightened appreciation of organizations as situated within and heavily influenced by their broader environment. With these concerns on the minds of managers, it was not long before organization and management theorists of all types began to research the relationship of the organization to the environment (Emery & Trist, 1965; Katz & Kahn, 1966). The underlying assumption of this approach is that organizations operating under norms of rationality seek stability and certainty in their dealing with the elements that constitute their "relevant" environment (Thompson, 1967). Environmental fluidity and complexity (Emery & Trist, 1965) explained significant variation in organizational designs and characteristics (Burns & Stalker, 1961; Lawrence & Lorsch, 1967; Aiken & Hage, 1968). More importantly, cooperative relationships with other organizations were an effective tool for organizations to manage resource dependencies and help shape their environments to their own advantage (Levin & White, 1961; Litwak & Hylton, 1962; Weick, 1969). This increased interdependence of organizations on each other

Figure 1 Three disciplinary lenses in the study of networks in public management and policy

increased attention to the importance of resource-supplying organizations in a specific or *focal organization's* environment.

Networks emerged as a management concern during this early period principally as attributes of organizations. William Evan (1965) proposed the organization set as a more specific network model of the focal organization's environment, the focal organization being the organization that you are studying. The set included all the actors (e.g., suppliers, customers, unions, distributors, trade associations, government agencies, and client groups) that provided inputs to the organization or took the outputs of the organization. The organizations in the set constituted the organization's network. Network management strategies, such as mergers, joint or collaborative ventures, and board interlocks, were viewed as tools that firms used to minimize or strategically manage resource dependency relationships in their environment (Pfeffer & Salancik, 1978).

Research on organizational sets diffused into public administration (e.g., Aldrich, 1976) and the term organization set was replaced with the term interorganizational network. The term interorganizational network was used to describe a set of exchange relationships among a collection of organizations. Actors in authoritative positions in organizations in the network negotiate the terms and duration of these relationships. Benson (1975) brought theories of power and politics to bear on interorganizational networks within the context of a network's political economy. Ostrom, Parks, and Whitaker (1974) introduced "public service industries" as a framework to conduct comparative research on interorganizational networks.

Around the same time, a somewhat different phenomenon caught the attention of organizational scholars. Multi-organizational entities, referred to variously as alliances, coalitions, collaboratives, consortiums, networks, and partnerships, were becoming increasingly prevalent as subjects of research. To distinguish them from organizational sets, multi-organizational entities were termed "action sets" as a way of understanding purposeful, goal-directed behavior by a collection of organizations that create a second-order organization to represent them collectively (Aldrich & Whetten, 1981). Action sets emerge when three or more parties discover that they have more to gain by collaboration on an issue than by pursuing independent courses of action (Mayer, 1972, pp. 135–136). They usually start as a group of actors who join for a time-limited purpose. The group then will either dissolve or develop into a more differentiated form such as the federation that assigns some limited functions to a centralized body (Warren, 1967), pursuing desired policy outcomes in the manner of trade associations or labor federations. The action set concept was a purpose-oriented network and the theoretical predecessor to the concept of whole networks (Provan et al., 2007), goal-directed networks (Saz-Carranza & Ospina, 2011), and CGRs (Emerson & Nabatchi, 2015).

The Evolution of the Policy
Lens on Networks

The evolution of the policy lens on networks is rooted in a disciplinary perspective from political science and driven by two key ambitions. The first was a desire to develop tools and theories that could explain policy as a product of the interactions between a multitude of actors (Klijn & Koppenjan, 2000). The second was an effort to advance theory concerning the development and maintenance of institutions of governance (Kiser & Ostrom, 1982; Sabatier, 1987). Both desires exist in relational studies in political science going back many years.

Policy Subsystems: The tradition of viewing policy outcomes as the product of a complex array of actors and their connections to one another, both formal and informal, dates to the New Deal in the United States (Griffith 1939). In the postwar years, this relational model became known as subsystem politics, a politics in the pluralist tradition that cuts across institutional boundaries and functions with varying degrees of autonomy from the larger political system which it depends upon for its legitimacy (Fritchler, 1969). The essential characteristics of this form of politics are "... a complex problem to be dealt with and the coalescing of power among those who have the interest or the yen to deal with it" (Cater, 1964, p. 20). The "complex problems" relate to a specialized policy domain like education, health care, housing, or national defense.[2] Initially, this work focused on a comparatively narrow conception of pertinent actors known as "iron triangles" that consisted of an issue like housing policy and the interests that viewed housing as their domain; namely a congressional committee or subcommittee, a government bureau, and an interest group like the Home Builders Association. However, scholars came to realize most subsystems were more extensive than the iron triangle and open to multiple committees and subcommittees, government agencies, and interest groups, in other words, an "issue network" (Heclo, 1978). The normative theme underlying these studies was the power imbalance of some subsystem participants compared to others that were characterized as plural elitism (Mills, 1959). It favored elites and insiders who were in it for the long haul over political hobbyists and the occasionally outraged. In an institutional sense, the lines that delineated actors in theories of subsystem politics became increasingly blurred

---

[2] In most cases, a policy domain is subdivided. In the education domain, there are different subsystems for higher education, K-12 education, educational equity, and school lunches.

between branches and levels of government as well as between lobbies and professional groups.

Policy Networks: Subsystem politics eventually gave way to policy networks. The concept of a policy network offered a better mousetrap that brought a measure of order and systematic rigor to what was largely descriptive, observational social science. The network perspective began to emerge when scholars observed that programs funded by government grants had a relational element to them, creating linkages binding program professionals and their professional associations together through all three layers of the US Federal System into what the Advisory Commission on Intergovernmental Relations called "vertical functional autocracies" (Davidson, 1974, p. 105).[3] This vertical element of policy subsystems became prominent during the Johnson and Nixon Administrations with programs designed in Washington but implemented in 50 states and 10,000 localities. From the Safe Streets Act to the Community Mental Health Act, these programs created management challenges for the governors and mayors who were responsible for implementing these programs and who needed to work with state and federal administrators in specialized policy silos who did not report to them.

By the late 1970s and early 1980s, democratic governments in Europe and the United States had created numerous programs and policies that made the policy world dense (Wildavsky, 1979). There was an increasing need to understand what came to be called policy networks and develop theories to provide guidance on how to design, manage, and evaluate them. Challenges in cross-sector and cross-level policy implementation started to be conceived of as "network problems" (Hanf et al., 1978; Scharpf, 1978). Political scientists studying policy implementation began to emphasize the management challenges inherent in top-down implementation executed through long causal chains of actors at various levels of government who had different preferences (Pressman & Wildavsky, 1973; Sabatier & Mazmanian, 1979). In response to these implementation challenges within a top-down approach, Elmore (1979) argued that scholars studying implementation were starting at the wrong end of the policy chain. He argued that you should look at what was happening at the local level and ask what needed to be done to make the policy more effective at every subsequent step upward in the implementation chain. Elmore called this "mapping backwards." Unlike Pressman and Wildavsky (1973), this was a bottom-up rather than top-down approach. While in many ways, this was

---

[3] The only current work in this area is *Forging Bureaucratic Autonomy* by Daniel Carpenter. He uses both historical and network analysis to argue that in the Progressive Era in the United States, meso level bureaucrats who had a high degree of expertise and political skill could sometimes forge a degree of bureaucratic autonomy from congressional oversight using interest groups and professional associations as counterweights to congressional committees.

a thought experiment, it had an impact on many scholars studying implementation. Sabatier (1987) became a convert as his work on the advocacy coalition framework applies policy subsystems and policy implementation to decision-making at the point at which policy is delivered.

Service Implementation Networks: Policy scholars and management scholars struggled with how to understand service implementation networks. It was hard to understand how the policy and organizational dimensions of implementation fit together in a multi-organizational network. Hjern and Porter (1981) solved this conceptual dilemma by positing "implementation structures" as units of analysis where an "organizational logic" competed with a "program logic" in every organization and program engaged in service delivery.

The Evolution of the Community Planning Lens on Networks

The community planning perspective has a normative lens that seeks to make community planning more effective and responsive. It reflects a distinct orientation toward networks that is anchored in place-based approaches to complex problems. One might question the inclusion of the community planning lens in a book on a network taxonomy, as one feature of this disciplinary lens is the notable absence of the use of the term "network." However, scholars anchored in the community planning perspective are interested in groups of three or more actors who unite to accomplish that which no one actor could accomplish alone. They tend to use terms like multi-sectoral partnerships, community collaboratives, coalitions, and alliances rather than networks to describe the entity. The community planning lens differs from both the organization and policy lenses in its place-based, problem-centric agenda. This agenda evolved during the late 1980s and early 1990s, strongly influenced by an interest in community-based collaboration and power-sharing relationships in health and human services as well as a growing emphasis on collaborative arrangements between state and nonstate actors to address environmental conflicts. Around the same time, health and human services saw increasing interest in widespread federal, state, and philanthropic initiatives that promoted community collaboration as a vehicle for addressing all manner of social ills.

One key influence in conceptualizing networks as place-based, problem-centric entities was the work of Emery and Trist. In 1965, Fred Emery and Eric Trist articulated a framework conceptualizing environmental complexity. Trist (1983) argued that societal problems were too complex to be managed by single organizations and should instead be managed by organizational domains comprised of multiple organizations and agencies linked together through their mutual goal interdependence with the meta-problem. Meta-problems were

conceived of as multidimensional problems, which cut across traditional bureaucratic silos, industries, and sectors (Emery & Trist, 1965 Trist, 1983). Trist
argued that organization and coordination of the domain were critical to making
progress on complex social issues. He further spoke of the importance of
"domain-based, inter-organizational competence" (p. 270) and the role of
referent organizations. Problem domains emphasized problem definition over
policy outcome as the anchoring concept and could encompass all manner of
actors across sectors deemed relevant to the problem.

Trist's ideas appear to have been influenced by his colleague at Wharton, Ed
Freeman, whose seminal book on stakeholder theory (1984) came out about the
same time. Whereas Trist was focused on stakeholders who could add or
subtract value with concern to a given problem domain, Freeman was focused
on stakeholders in relation to the individual organization. In both cases, the
notion of interdependence among organizations and agencies, and that these
interdependencies had societal implications, was a central thesis. Freemans's
stakeholder theory became particularly relevant for the community planning
lens of networks as it provided theoretical justification for engagement with the
private sector in collaborative efforts with public and nonprofit organizations to
address social ills that were attributable, in part, to the role of capitalism in
society.

Meanwhile, in the planning world, Horst Rittel and Melvin Webber published
their influential *Dilemmas in a General Theory of Planning* (1973), which
introduced the delightful term "wicked problems" to the academic nomenclature and offered an explanation for why gold standard, evidence-based, planning processes were habitually unsuccessful in confronting certain social issues.
They went on to argue that rationalized planning systems, based on applied
scientific decision processes, assume goals and desired outcomes are clear and
agreed upon – a condition that is rarely true in addressing societal problems.
They argued that wicked problems are problems in which there is no clear
problem definition, no stopping rule, no definitive definition of a successful
outcome or test for determining success even if it exists, no opportunity for
consequence-free trial and error learning, and no exhaustible set of solutions,
root causes, or plausible remedies. The role of the "publics" as both critics and
stakeholders of professional program design was front and center in Rittell and
Webber's writing. This work was widely embraced by scholars as further
justification of the need for technological advancements in the creation of multistakeholder, community-engaged, collaborative forums and processes for
addressing complex problems. Alter and Hage (1993), Friend and Hickling
(1987), Eden and Ackermann (1998), Gray (1989), Huxham and Vangen
(2013), and Bryson and Crosby (1992) responded to this call by creating

a range of frameworks and models defining the requisite conditions, intervening factors, dynamics, and outcomes of collaborative problem-solving processes involving a diverse set of stakeholders associated with a common issue of concern.

Collectively, these developments contributed to an orientation to networks that was place-based, system-oriented, and problem-centered. This contrasted sharply with the policy lens' view of networks that was problem-centered but oriented toward how regulations and funding flow through levels of government creating a vertical political economy. It also contrasts with the organizational lens view of networks that is system-oriented but centered on how an inter-organizational network is managed and governed.

Conclusion

In this section, we considered three disciplinary lenses that have shaped the study of networks in public management and policy – organizational, policy, and community planning. Each of these disciplinary lenses has made a significant contribution to our understanding of all three classes of networks: structural, system, and purpose oriented. These lenses provide scholars in public management and policy with different (although not mutually exclusive) ways of understanding and conducting research on networks.

As demonstrated by this section, the study of networks in public management and policy has drawn from, and been informed by, a rich intellectual heritage that has spanned multiple disciplines and evolved over many decades. Organizational, policy, and community planning perspectives on networks are each anchored in different pursuits, situated in the dominant concerns of the disciplines over time. Different disciplines looked to networks to try and solve different types of problems that were situated at different levels of analysis. Understanding the preoccupations of these forbearers can help scholars today to understand both the differences between the classes of networks (structural-oriented, system-oriented, and purpose-oriented) as well as better appreciate variances that exist within the class. We argue that in understanding this history of networks, we are better positioned as a field to benefit from the rich diversity of perspectives offered both across and within classes. In the next three sections, we now turn our attention to offering a more in-depth examination of each of the three classes of networks: structural oriented (Section 3), system oriented (Section 4), and purpose oriented (Section 5).

3 Structural-Oriented Networks

Our first class of networks – structural-oriented networks – is perhaps the least commonly encountered class within the field of public management and policy. This is not because structural-oriented networks are not prominent in public and nonprofit contexts. On the contrary, they are ubiquitous! In fact, we struggle to think of a single area of scholarship that does not encompass a multitude of structural-oriented networks. The reason they are less encountered is simply because we, as a discipline, tend to not focus heavily on them, seeing greater theoretical and practical consequences in the system- and purpose-oriented networks. However, as we will demonstrate in this section, structural-oriented networks allow us to gain insight into key micro-dynamics that can be present in networks of any class.

Structural-oriented networks are representations of social structure with arbitrary analyst-imposed boundaries; **these networks are delineated from the other classes in that the collection of actors and their ties are not presumed to represent any higher-order entity**. These networks are comprised of nodes and edges.[4] Nodes refer to actors with agency to form or delete ties with other actors. Edges refer to the existence of a linkage or relationship between two nodes. This linkage can be anything (e.g., trust, friendship, contracts, kinship, coauthorship) and is limited only by the analyst's imagination. Whereas system-oriented networks are created by analysts and existentially linked to the system they are deemed to represent (see Section 4), and purpose-oriented networks are self-actualized entities created by their members (see Section 5), structural-oriented networks do not represent a superordinate entity, they are simply snapshots of social structure. As such, this class of networks is delineated from the other classes based on its overriding preoccupation with the component-building blocks of networks from a graph-theoretic perspective, namely nodes and edges. Put simply, a "network" within this class of networks is anything that can be construed to consist of nodes and edges. However, structural-oriented networks fundamentally differ from other classes in that the population of nodes in structural-oriented networks does not attempt to represent membership of a higher-order entity.

Scholarship on structural-oriented networks can generally be delineated into *dyadic* and *ego-centric* network studies (see Figure 2). Dyadic network studies focus on the edges, seeking to understand the patterns and consequences of different edge configurations for the evolution of the network over time. In comparison, ego-centric studies focus on the nodes and seek to understand the

---

[4] See Galloway and Thacker (2007) for a more expanded conception of networks, which includes structural components (i.e., nodes, edges) as well as process components (protocols and flows).

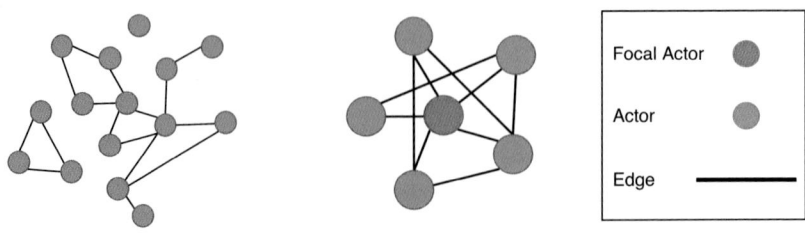

Dyadic Network   Ego-Centric Network

Figure 2 Ego-centric versus dyadic structural-oriented networks
This figure represents the comparison of an ego-centric network and a dyadic network

consequences of the composition and patterning of a given node's ties to other actors. Berry et al. (2004) attribute this division back to the work of Mitchell (1969) who was one of the first to distinguish ego-centered approaches to understanding networks versus those focused on understanding the qualities of dyads (e.g., reciprocity, intensity) and their macro patterns such as density, reachability, and cliques within an interconnected population of dyads.

Nodes and Edges versus Governance Root Metaphors of Networks

Conceiving of structural-oriented networks can be awkward for scholars trained in the tradition which viewed networks as a form of governance where networks are deemed to have some overarching purpose (in purpose-oriented networks) or system function (in system-oriented networks). This highlights the existence of two competing root metaphors of networks which are useful in understanding the differences in the three network classes and specifically in understanding structural-oriented networks.

Abstract concepts like "network" emerge into literatures in time and space and reflect the historical preoccupations of their originators. Root metaphors reflect the core understanding of a concept and frequently transcend disciplines. These metaphors encompass the generally unspoken assumptions about what a network is, why it is relevant, and how the concept should be applied. Over time disciplinary literatures converge and diverge, metaphors can become mixed and yet retain a distinct linage. **We argue that how a scholar conceptualizes the concept of a network can be traced to two distinct root metaphors: (1) networks as nodes and edges and (2) network as governance form.** Structural-oriented networks are firmly anchored in the nodes and edges tradition.

Networks as Nodes and Edges: The nodes and edges tradition emerges from graph theory and coevolved with the development of the tools and techniques of social network analysis (SNA). In this sociometric perspective, a network refers to any collection of three or more "actors" referred to as nodes that are linked together by some form of "relation" described as edges. An actor has some degree of agency to interact with other actors. People, organizations, groups, computers, animals – all can be actors. Further, what might constitute a "relation" or "edge" can be ties of friendship, kinship, information, resource exchange, and contracts, all facilitated by trust built upon reciprocity. Watts (2004) referred to this as "The New Science of Networks" and focused heavily on the methodological and mathematical challenges associated with modeling meaningful characteristics of social structure such as triadic closure, structural holes, significant subgroups, and network clusters. As stated by Watts (2004), "[w]ithout doubt, the structure of real-world networks, and the evolution thereof, are legitimate scientific problems the general resolution of which presents us with substantial modeling and empirical challenges" (p. 256).

Much of the nodes and edges tradition of network research is rooted in sociology and anthropology (Watts, 2004). It began in the 1930s with the work of Jacob Moreno (1934). Moreno created what he called "sociometry" that captured the relationships between individuals in graph format. In this manner, it was possible to tell who was connected to whom in terms of various types of relations. There was relational work in the social sciences between the 1930's to the 1960s, but it had little influence on mainstream disciplinary research in sociology and political science. It wasn't until the work of Harrison White at Harvard in the 1970s (e.g., White, 1970; White et al., 1976) that social networks emerge as a theory of society based on human relationships that provides an alternative explanation of human behavior other than the nominal categories of race, class, and gender (Freeman, 2004).[5] By focusing on relationships, social network analysis provided an alternative to methodological individualism as a way of understanding human behavior. In addition to his contributions to theory and methods, White began training graduate students in social network analysis, producing a considerable body of work that seeded the modern development of the field. In his history of the field of social network analysis, Freeman (2004, p. 3) asserts that after a long gestation period (1930s–1970s), the study of social networks has been integrated into a research paradigm characterized by a focus on ties linking social actors, an emphasis on systematic empirical data, the use of graphic network imagery as a diagnostic

---

[5] Social network analysis complements nominal categories in providing evidence for how powerful race, class and gender are by demonstrating how homophily provides evidence that "birds of a feather" is the first principle of social network analysis.

tool, and the use of computational models. White's teaching and research were influential, in part, because his program of research was broader than the small group studies that had proceeded with it.[6]

Other early developments in structural-oriented network studies included "The Strength of Weak Ties" (Granovetter, 1973), one of the most celebrated papers in sociology for linking levels of social analysis. Simmel's theory of social triads looked at the power of three connected actors as possessing sociologically unique qualities not explained by the aggregation of their dyadic components. Laumann et al. (1978) advocated using community structure as an aggregate network of interorganizational relations, and Breiger (1976) demonstrated the duality of persons and groups in networks. These are examples of many innovative uses of theory and methods reflecting the edges and nodes root metaphor of networks.

Networks as Governance Form: Where the edges and node metaphor viewed networks as empirically measurable representations of social structure. The networks as governance root metaphor used the concept of networks to refer to an abstract form of collective action that is neither market capitalism nor hierarchical command and control. This metaphor emerged out of the disciplines of economics, sociology, and political science in the mid-twentieth century as a way to characterize the ways in which human societies accomplish collective aims.

Dahl and Lindblom (1953) proposed four basic processes for collective action: market system, hierarchy, polyarchy, and bargaining. The latter two terms were similar to the related concept of polycentricity coined by Polanyi (1951). He argued that, particularly in problem spaces with multiple decision centers and complex cause and effect relations, outcomes must not be imposed in a top-down manner; rather effective systems of governance must allow free interaction among agents in the trial-and-error pursuit of common ideals. Polycentricity became central in the work of Elinor and Vincent Ostrom at their workshop on Political Theory and Policy Analysis at University of Indiana, Bloomington. The concept of networks naturally emerged in this scholarship as a useful concept to characterize the collection of actors who enacted these processes and participated in these decision centers.[7]

A second branch of scholarship anchored in the networks as governance root metaphor emerged at the boundary of economics and organizational theory, in the work of Oliver Williamson (1975) whose theory of transaction cost economics argues that organizations have three choices in procuring assets needed

---

[6]   Much of this section is based on Pachucki, & Lewis. (2017).

[7]   One of the earliest uses of the term network in a governance context was in Ostrom, Parks, & Whitaker. (1974).

to produce a good and service: (1) they can make the asset in-house governed by top-down bureaucratic hierarchy, (2) they can purchase it on the market, governed by price, or (3) they can do something in the middle which involves repeated exchanges and the development of trust to reduce transaction costs. This latter form Williamson simply referred to as a "hybrid" (1991). Similarly, Ouchi (1991) used the concept of "clans" to describe an alternative governance form to markets and bureaucracy. Rather than prices or control, clans utilize common values and beliefs along with traditions as a means of control. **A key point is that a social choice that does not clearly fall into a market or a hierarchy can be made through an alternative governance form that relies on reciprocity, collective norms, and trust to do the work of prices or command.** It was not until the work of Powell (1991) that we find the term "network" used to refer to this form of economic organization.

Delineating Characteristics of Structural-Oriented Networks

By the mid-1990s, the term "network" was becoming more prevalent in the academic literature; however, even in these early years, scholars were using the term quite differently. This is because these two competing root metaphors offer different prescriptions of what might be thought of as a "network." In the **nodes and edges tradition, variation in the structure of relations and their associated antecedents and consequences is what is of paramount concern to the analyst. The goal is to identify consequential network structures in the abstract** (Berry et al., 2004). Who the nodes or actors are or what system or entity they represent is secondary, if not irrelevant. In other words, a structural hole is a structural hole (see Burt, 1995), no matter where it is observed. This is in contrast with the governance metaphor where the theorized processes of governance within a given context are of principal concern, and the network concept is justified only to the extent it captures the relevant actors associated with some system of interest (see system-oriented networks; Section 4). This frequently unappreciated difference in emphasis linked to these root metaphors has led to many confusing and frustrating conversations between network scholars, not recognizing they represent two different traditions in the network world.

Structural-oriented networks are snapshots of social structure and as such, they have no meaning, identity, or existence outside of their consequences for the network components. Different from the other two classes, these networks are not presumed to represent any higher-order entity. Structural components of these networks consist of nodes (actors) and edges (ties). As such, structural-oriented networks can either be *ego-centric* or *dyadic* in nature. Ego-centric networks are networks that consist of the attributes of a focal actor (Wasserman

Table 1 Delineating Characteristics of Structural-Oriented Networks

---

➤ Network is an attribute of a node or emergent consequence of patterns of dyadic tie formation

➤ Network is theoretically boundless and limited only by arbitrary cut offs imposed by the analyst

➤ Inclusion of actors in the network is based entirely on relational approaches associated with an arbitrary initial sample of actors

➤ The "network" is not presumed to represent any higher order entity or system of interest

---

& Faust, 1994). All ties within an ego-centric network are linked back to a focal actor (ego), either directly or indirectly through one or more brokerage relationships. Dyadic structural networks are emergent patterns of structure that are a consequence of dyadic tie creation or deletion between actors. In ego-centric networks, the focus is on the consequences of network structure for actors within the network. In dyadic networks, the focus is on the emergent structural patterns of tie formation and their consequences for future tie creation or deletion.

Structural-oriented networks are conceptually very different from our other two classes of networks principally due to their almost boundary-less nature (see related discussion on scale-free networks in Barabasi & Bonabeau, 2003; Broido & Clauset, 2019; and Holme, 2019). While analysts will use sampling procedures and decision rules to limit the number of nodes and/or edges that are taken into consideration in their analysis of structural-oriented networks, the network boundaries created by these decision rules are driven largely by feasibility and sampling logic rather than any sociologically meaningful boundary. For example, it is common in studies of ego networks to sample alters (actors connected to ego) within one degree of separation from the ego. This means that the analyst would seek to capture all direct ties to focal actor A as well as all indirect ties through one broker. In other words, if actor A is friends with actor B and actor B is friends with actor C but not actor A, both actors B and C would be considered part of A's ego network. Actors connected to C but not A or B would not be considered part of the network. However, this boundary is entirely arbitrary and imposed by the analyst. Albeit potentially difficult in many situations, it is theoretically feasible to capture ego networks at 3rd, 4th, or 5th degrees of separation (friends of friends of friends of friends) as demonstrated in the scholarship on small-world networks (Watts, 2004; Opsahl et al., 2017). The actual boundaries of structural-oriented networks associated with people theoretically extend out to the boundaries of interconnected human populations.

When scholars talk about networks in public management and policy, it is our sense that they generally are referring to either purpose- or system-oriented networks. However, a recent review by Siciliano and colleagues (2021) revealed a significant amount of scholarship dedicated to structural-oriented networks. Here we review some of the major themes associated with this work.

Tie Formation in Structural-Oriented Networks

A relatively commonly encountered theme in public management and policy scholarship is studies of tie formation (for review, see Siciliano et al., 2021). Policy and management scholars are interested in developing a general theory to predict who collaborates with whom (e.g., Atouba & Shumate, 2015; Nohrstedt & Bodin, 2019), who contracts with whom (e.g., Hugg, 2019), who becomes friends with whom (e.g., Tulin et al., 2019), who donates money to whom (e.g., Herzog & Yang, 2018), and who communicates with whom (Park & Rethmeyer, 2014).

Many of these studies are embedded within system-oriented networks. They seek to describe how lower-order structural network dynamics influence the outcomes of a given system of interest. For example, Park and Rethemeyer (2014) extend their earlier work on Newstatia ABE policy network (see Rethemeyer & Hatmaker, 2008). The ABE policy network was bounded by the authors as actors engaged in "Decisions that affect the funding or regulation of organizations that provide educational services to individuals 16 years of age or older who are seeking to raise their reading, writing, and/or computational skills to a level closer to that of a high school graduate in a defined geographic area." (Park & Rethemeyer, 2014, p. 354)

Park and Rethemeyer (2014) used Exponential Random Graph models (ERGMs) to estimate the factors, specifically resource dependency relationships, that predict communication ties within this policy network. While the intent of this article was to advance a more general theory about predictors of tie formation, the "network" of interest was clearly conceptualized and operationalized as a system-oriented network. As such, it serves as a nice illustration of an investigation of structural network dynamics in a system-oriented network.

However, studies of tie formation of relevance to public management and policy can also be carried out in structural-oriented networks where boundaries are arbitrary. For example, both Siciliano (2016) and Nisar and Maroulis (2017) sought to understand the network characteristics that promoted advice giving and receiving among teachers. Specifically, they were interested in the influence of factors such as homophily, level of expertise, and triadic closure in the selection of peers in advice-giving networks. In order to test their hypotheses, the authors utilized data from a sample of teachers. The teachers were not selected because they reflected the key personnel in a system of interest. The authors did not seek to represent these teachers as system-level actors. There was no purpose-oriented network to which these teachers consciously affiliated. Rather, these teachers were selected because they were viewed as a theoretically interesting sample of street-level bureaucrats. For example, Nisar and Maroulis (2017) argued that "[a]nalyzing the workplace relations of teachers has the additional benefit of providing a context in which individuals often access resources, particularly tacit expertise about the complex task of teaching, through informal social networks." In other words, the "network" was of consequence only because of its importance to the actors within the network and their patterns of tie formation.

Tie Performance in Structural-Oriented Networks

A related area of inquiry where structural-oriented networks may be encountered is in efforts to generate general theory about the factors that support or undermine the effectiveness of network ties. Again, these efforts commonly occur in the context of purpose- or system-oriented networks as part of a larger agenda to explain system or group-level outcomes (e.g. Nowell & Steelman, 2013, D'Andreta et al., 2016). However, it is not uncommon to investigate the performance of ties in purely structural-oriented networks. For example, Ofem, Arya, and Borgatti (2018) investigated measures of effectiveness of 298 dyadic collaborations between ninety-eight economic development organizations. Network characteristics such as centrality, mutual dependence, and structural dependence were modeled as predictors of the effectiveness of a collaboration between dyads. However, the boundaries of the network were defined by the analysts as the population of not-for-profit economic development organizations operating in eastern Kentucky. This network was not presented as reflecting a larger system of interest nor were these organizations part of a purpose-oriented network. They were simply a theoretically interesting population of organizations with patterns of collaborative ties to one another. Further, the boundaries drawn around this population of organizations were largely arbitrary and focused entirely on homogeneity of nodal form (economic development organizations) and geography (located in a specific part of Kentucky). In other words, they reflected a structural-oriented network of theoretical interest. In another example, Hegele (2018) examined power as operationalized by centrality in communication networks among 171 local government leaders in Germany. As with the Oftem et al. (2018) network, this network was chosen simply because it reflected a theoretically interesting sample of government actors who were connected through communication networks and as such offered an information-rich context to understand tie and actor characteristics that predict who is likely to gain more power in interconnected networks.

Learning and Diffusion of Innovation in Structural-Oriented Networks

Networks have long been viewed as the vehicles through which information and innovation diffuse in society (Rogers, 1962). Diffusion of innovation and learning through networks are topics of keen interest to the field of public management and policy (Tasselli, 2015; D'Andreta et al., 2016; Kammerer & Namhata, 2018; Vantaggiato, 2018). This is an area where structural-oriented networks are commonly encountered. For example, Kammerer and Namhata (2018) investigated the ego-network characteristics of countries as one of the explanatory factors in understanding whether countries adopt climate change policies. The network in this investigation is a classic example of structural-oriented ego network. There is no larger system being represented and the counties are connected through dyadic ties rather than collectively all affiliated to some self-actualized group (see Section 5). The sample of countries was chosen because they represented a theoretically interesting sample of interconnected actors – in this case, sovereign countries – from which to investigate the consequences of social structure on the policy adoption behavior of actors within the network. The network is meaningful only because it has consequences for the actors within it. Another example is that of Tasselli (2015). In this case, the author investigates knowledge transfer within a structural-oriented network of 118 healthcare professionals sampled from a single department in a hospital. Arguably, this setting could be viewed as an information-rich setting for examining hospital departments as system-oriented networks, with a focus on understanding how micro-dynamics of network interactions contribute to, or detract from, departmental level performance. However, as described in more detail in Section 4, system-oriented networks are defined by the analyst. This would have required the analyst to establish the boundaries of the "system" that leads to departmental performance and then identify the associated network of actors associated with that system. This was not Tasselli's (2015) intent. Rather, Tasselli's intent was to study this sample of interconnected actors within this department as a structural-oriented network to understand patterns of knowledge transfer between doctors and nurses. The author was specifically seeking to understand how different positions and patterns lead to different outcomes for both actors (which actors get more information) and ties (how communication flows). System-level (i.e., departmental) implications of these micro-dynamics were alluded to but not the focus.

Organizational Network Advantage and Performance

Last, scholars in public management and policy are invested in understanding the factors that promote efficiency and effectiveness of public and nonprofit organizations. Networks are increasingly viewed as a critical piece of the puzzle in understanding organizational advantage and performance (Burt et al., 2013). This area of interest emphasizes the importance of recognizing that organizations are embedded within structural-oriented networks, linked to other organizations, agencies, and stakeholders through a myriad of information exchanges, contracting relationships, resource dependencies, and professional affiliations. Xu and Saxton (2019) explore the implications of this connectivity via social media engagement. Specifically, they examined a Twitter peer network that was constructed based on follower/followee relationships among a sample of 198 community foundations, focusing on how Twitter engagement strategies related to indicators of organizational social capital within the peer network. In another example, Faulk and colleagues (Faulk et al., 2016) investigate the consequences of ego-network characteristics of interlocking board members for a sample of nonprofits and foundations and their success in obtaining foundation grant dollars. They found that network effects did help explain organizational success at obtaining foundation grants partially mediated by organizational history and financial capacity. Finally, the work of O'Toole and Meier (2003) looks at organizational outcomes for school districts as predicted indirectly by bi-partite ego networks of district superintendents in terms of their networking behavior with different classes of external stakeholders (school board members, local business leaders, other school superintendents, state legislators, and the state education agency). They found this networking behavior was positively and significantly related to district outcomes such as parent involvement, community support, and school board support.

Conclusion

As illustrated by the themes already mentioned, structural-oriented networks are everywhere. Anywhere actors are connected to other actors through some type of relationship, a structural-oriented network exists. Consideration of these networks highlights that organizations, agencies, programs, and people do not operate in isolation. They are embedded within a web of relationships and one's position within this social space has consequences. How central actors are, how densely connected their ties are to other actors, the extent to which ties are direct or are heavily brokered, whether friends of friends tend to become friends over time, or whether the competitor of your competitor becomes your collaborator are part of the micro-dynamics that can help explain a myriad of individual and relational outcomes between actors. These networks reflect social structure that can have consequences for the actors involved as well as creating the conditions that predict where and how new ties will form, and existing ties may be terminated. Expanding our understanding of the micro-dynamics of networks can help us better understand our social world, advancing a more complex understanding of networked environments in all classes of networks.

4 System-Oriented Networks

Consider the questions: How does food get from farm to table? What is the network of actors associated with its production and distribution? How is this network structured and organized? How do actors relate to, coordinate, or organize within this network? What institutions govern this network? Who is relevant to understanding this network? Who is not? How might these characteristics of the network help explain the outcomes that we observe?

These types of questions are of central concern to those who seek to understand and intervene within our second class of networks in public management and policy: system-oriented networks. **System-oriented networks are networks conceptualized by a network analyst to represent the population of actors, and their interactions, germane to some system of interest, generally associated with a policy, program, or problem domain.** Thus, the unit of theory in system-oriented networks generally refers to a network associated with an issue of public concern or public policy. A good example is the contemporary farm-to-school movement " . . . described as a system comprised of discrete actors operated at varying levels of geographic scale, social sector, and network function" (Conner et al., 2011, p. 133). In this example, the system is defined by the production, processing, distribution, regulation, and consumption of local food to institutional consumers – in particular, local schools. The associated unit of theory is the network comprised of the actors who are deemed by the network analyst to play a significant role in a farm-to-school network. While this example is a recent one, this type of system-oriented network analysis is among the earliest type of network studies in public management and policy. In Europe, early system-oriented network studies include work by Hanf, Hjern, and Porter (1978) on a comparative study of worker training systems in West Germany and Sweden, theoretical work by Scharpf (1978), and the work of Hjern and Porter (1981) on the nature of interorganizational policy making. In the United States, efforts to map networks associated with policy areas were introduced in the tradition of organizational sociology (Zald, 1970) and organization theory (Evan, 1972), including system-oriented network research by Milward (1982), Milward and Wamsley (1985), and Sabatier (1987). After the first conference was convened at Indiana University's Workshop on Political Theory and Policy Analysis in 1981, many of these European and American scholars came together over six summers at a variety of conference settings in Europe. While not typically thought of as network scholars, the work of Elinor and Vincent Ostrom, frequent attendees at these conferences, influenced both the Europeans and Americans. Investigations into system-oriented networks have proliferated in recent years, spanning

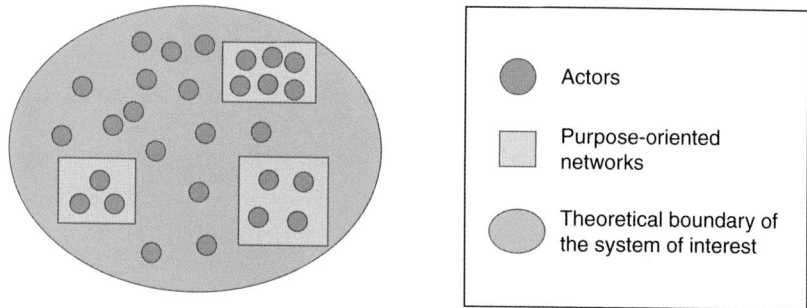

Figure 3 Visualizing actors and purpose-oriented networks as embedded within system-oriented networks

everything from efforts to understand network dynamics of actors engaged in managing watersheds within a given region (e.g., Lubell & Fulton, 2008) to the pattern of relationships among actors engaged in a response to a disaster (e.g., Kapucu & Garayev, 2016). As shown in Figure 3, system-oriented networks can be conceived of to include a diverse array of "actors" ranging from individuals to organizations to purpose-oriented networks (see Section 5).

A delineating feature of the system-oriented network is that they are **a conceptualization of a network analyst – the person, or persons, who conceive of the network**. **The network analyst defines the network using a set of decision rules justified based on their theoretical importance for understanding some systemic outcome of interest.** This does not mean that the system-oriented network is not verifiable by an outside observer using the same set of decision rules, or that it has no empirically observable actors or connections between the actors. However, from the perspective of our taxonomy, the system-oriented network does not necessarily have a stable or agreed-upon identity and boundary outside of the imaginings of the analyst. In Section 1 we quoted Laumann et al. (1983) who referred to these networks as nominalist networks, stating that "[h]ere, the analyst self-consciously imposes a conceptual framework [of the network] constructed to serve his or her own analytic purposes" (p. 66). The analyst does this by way of applying decision rules, implicit or explicit, which define the actors who are relevant or not relevant to the system of interest and thus to the network. Analytical choices are present in the study of any class of networks. However, with system-oriented networks, boundary specification is particularly critical as different analysts, policy makers, or practitioners may consider the same policy, program, or program domain and yet conceptualize the relevant network of actors quite differently (Nowell et al., 2018).

History of Systems in Social Science

System-oriented networks represent a class of networks in which the conceptualization of a network is tied to preconceptions about the nature of a system that a network is deemed to represent. In this way, scholarship on system-oriented networks is linked to the traditions and methodologies associated with social science perspectives on systems. To understand the former, one must have some grounding in the latter. In the social sciences, systems thinking is dominated by an epistemological perspective that sees systems as a heuristic defined by the analyst's preconceptions and interests (Abson et al., 2017). Positionality of the analyst influences the prescribed boundaries and thus the nature of the system "observed." However, the way in which the system is formulated ought to be grounded in empirical referents (Friis et al., 2017). Kaplan (1964) calls this "reconstructed logic." Thus, an analyst immerses herself, for example, in the institutions involved in influencing or implementing mitigation initiatives to protect human settlements from sea-level rise in a specific geographic area and then tries to inductively construct a model of the policy system associated with sea-level mitigation outcomes.

Scholarship on systems in the social sciences is vast; at least as diverse and as challenging to characterize as scholarship on networks. However, most scholars agree it is fundamentally rooted in, and motivated by, critiques of reductionist thinking that dominated intellectualism up through the first half of the twentieth century (Hammond, 2002). Systems thinking includes a preoccupation with ideas such as relationships between parts and wholes, feedback loops, processes of emergence, hierarchical nesting of systems, and holism. Ludwig von Bertalanffy (1951) was one of the first to organize systems into a coherent whole under the umbrella of what he called "General Systems Theory." From there, more specialized perspectives were either developed or adapted from the biophysical sciences including work on socio-technical systems, social ecology, cybernetics, complexity theory, complex adaptive systems theory, and systems dynamics by interdisciplinary scholars like Ross Ashby (1956), Kenneth Boulding (1956), and Russell Ackoff and Fred Emery (1972). After seventy years, the core tenets of the systems approach have remained relatively constant across a diversity of approaches. Mingers and White (2010, p. 4) identify the following elements in system theory:

1. Viewing the situation holistically, as opposed to reductionistically, as a set of diverse interacting elements within an environment;
2. Recognizing that the relationships or interactions between elements are more important than the elements themselves in determining the behavior of the system;

3. Recognizing a hierarchy of levels of systems and the consequent ideas of properties emerging at different levels, and mutual causality both within and between levels;

4. Accepting, especially in social systems, that people will act in accordance with differing purposes or rationalities.

The Socially Constructed Nature of Systems

"System" is a term used to describe a collection of interacting or interdependent processes that collectively coproduce an outcome of interest. In public management and policy, we frequently speak of systems (the welfare system, the justice system, the education system, the healthcare system) as real entities, just as we speak of system-oriented networks as real entities. However, at their core, both systems and system-oriented networks are abstractions. Nominalism is a philosophy that questions whether abstractions can be thought of as real entities outside of the minds of those who conceive of them. We align ourselves with the perspective put forth by Tsoukas (2016) who argued for embracing an ontological duality that views systems as both enacted patterns of relations as well as relatively stable entities that result from such patterning. Thus, while our intent is not to contribute to a philosophical debate concerning the metaphysical properties of systems and their associated system-oriented networks, some consideration of where these abstractions come from and how they come to be understood is warranted.

It is important to recognize that systems do not exist independent of the outcome they are deemed to produce. Elements believed to comprise a system have an existence independent of a given outcome, but the system itself, as an entity, cannot. This is because one cannot speak of a system in any meaningful way without first clarifying "a system for *what*." In identifying the "what," the analyst identifies the outcome for which the system of interest is reasoned to produce. In doing so, the analyst literally calls a system into being as an entity. As such, it is somewhat problematic to view a system as an independent variable that creates outcomes in light of the fact that it is simultaneously *defined by its outcome*. The elements and relationships included and excluded from consideration are justified by their relevance to a stated outcome. Take for example the issue of homelessness. Certainly, most would agree that homelessness is a complex issue that lends itself well to systems thinking. However, the elements one might consider in understanding homelessness and responses to homelessness are vast. The elements one chooses will alter how one conceptualizes the issue. For example, is "the issue" of homelessness about how one transitions from having a house to not having a house? Is "the issue" about how one who is without a house addresses basic needs such as food, medical care, shelter, employment? Is "the issue" how one transitions from being without housing to obtaining stable housing? Each of these would suggest a somewhat different set of system elements to consider and subsequently, illuminate a potentially different set of network actors.

Once an outcome of interest is defined, the identification of the system that produces that outcome becomes another exercise in abstraction and human judgment. This activity involves two parts. The first part is identification of relevant elements – institutions or processes – and the second part is the identification of the relevant relationships among the elements in relation to the outcome. The goal here is to identify the most parsimonious collection of elements and relationships among them to explain variation in the outcome of interest. You can appreciate how, depending on the policy outcome(s) one considers or fails to consider, the elements deemed germane to the system may look different.

As our understanding of a phenomenon grows more complex, the array of potential elements and relationships among them increases beyond our ability to model. As such, applications of systems concepts and ideas in practice must simplify, through further abstraction, a limited number of elements and relationships. This is not problematic unless we forget that our simplifications are merely models constructed by us. **The problem arises when our decision rules for framing problems and identifying "relevant elements" become so institutionalized within disciplinary approaches that we lose our ability to critically evaluate these as analytic choices rather than realities.** If the elements of the system differ across analysts, the subsequent system-oriented network associated with the issue is also likely to vary (Nowell et al., 2017).

System-Oriented Networks

If systems are collections of interacting or interdependent processes that collectively coproduce an outcome of interest, their kinship with system-oriented networks becomes evident. Indeed, if systems are thought of as the processes that interact to produce an outcome, system-oriented networks can be thought of as the actors – an individual, group, organization, or purpose-oriented network – that influence the processes that effect an outcome of interest (see Figure 4).

In the system-oriented class of network scholarship, the network is thus a property of a larger preconceived system defined by the analyst. As with all classes of network scholarship, the term "actors" can be interpreted variously as anything that could be argued to have agency to exert influence into the system. While generally this is represented as individuals, groups, or organizations, this approach to network scholarship also lends itself to the conceptualization of

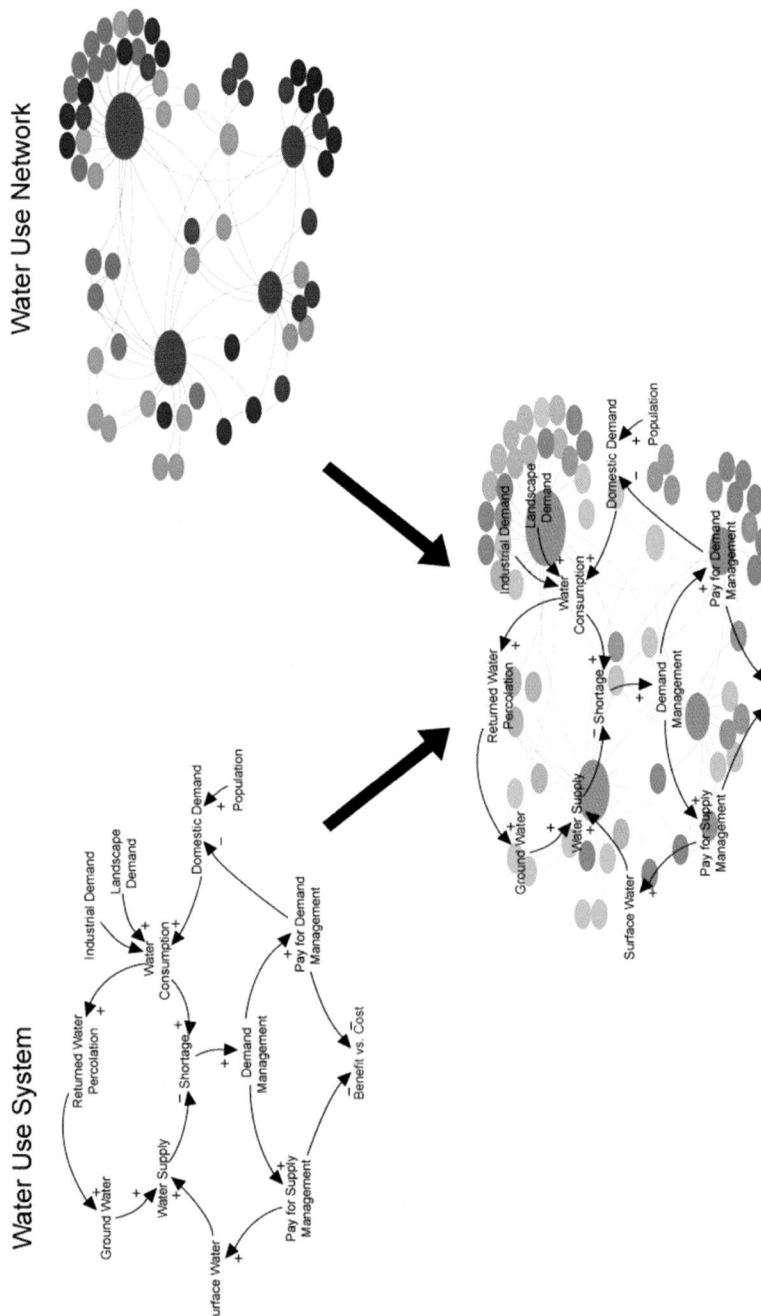

Figure 4 Illustration of the overlay of system elements and network actors
Source: Diagram adapted from Zarghami and Akbariyeh (2012)

Table 2 Delineating characteristics of system-oriented networks

➢ Like systems, the boundaries of what gets constituted as "the network" is determined by the analyst

➢ Justification of "the network" is bound to its representation of a system associated with some outcome of interest

➢ Criteria for inclusion or exclusion of actors from consideration of the network is tied to an actor's assumed relevancy to the system and can be independent of any network behavior

➢ Because both the system and subsequent network are conceptions of the analyst, there is no assumption that the actors themselves have any collective identity as being part of the network

➢ The network may include isolates – thus actors having no ties to the other actors in the network based on the relational attribute of interest

multimodal networks comprised of individuals linked together directly and indirectly through a variety of forums, events, and even purpose-oriented networks (Vantaggiato & Lubbell, 2020). The delineating characteristics of system-oriented networks are summarized in Table 2.

Apples to Apples: System-Oriented Network Scholarship in Public Management and Policy

Examples of system-oriented networks abound in the literature. Some of this literature is problem-centric; focusing on place-based challenges and attempting to map networks of actors engaged in, or relevant to, the management and/or governance of some problem or policy issue. Other studies are solution-centric and attempt to map actors associated with a complex policy implementation effort such as the network of actors associated with the disbursement of federal COVID relief and recovery funds or mental health services funded by state and federal agencies. In the sections that follow, we explore these types of networks in public management and policy.

Service Implementation Networks as System-Oriented Networks

A service implementation network is one where the payer, most often the government, picks the players. The players are those agencies who become contractors for the funder. Service implementation networks vary greatly on the degree to which they are integrated. This can vary from a series of "make or buy" decisions by an agency to a well-integrated network of service providers. Most scholarships on service implementation networks fit into the category of system-oriented networks. An early study of this nature was Provan and Milward (1995) "A Preliminary Theory of Interorganizational Network Effectiveness." The authors had a grant from the National Institute of Mental Health (NIMH) to do what was called a "systems study" of four community mental health systems in similarly sized cities in the United States. There was a normative belief among program officers at NIMH, analysts, and mental health professionals that integrated systems should perform more effectively for clients relative to systems that were not integrated. Integration referred to governance of some sort, although this was not defined on purpose. The Provan and Milward (1995) study had one fundamental research question: What, if any, is the relationship between the structure and context of mental health networks and their effectiveness? In the cases of the four cities where the study was conducted, the network was delineated based on the decision rule of agencies that provided mental health services or advocacy.

With four cities in the study, there was variation in the type of networks that delivered services to clients. The most effective site was Providence, Rhode Island, in which the system-oriented network was highly centralized around the Providence Center. This network was the most effective of the four sites. Providence Center operated a hub and spoke network in which the Providence Center was granted authority by the state to administer contracts to providers, thereby allowing them to mandate and enforce coordination and cooperation among providers. In another site, Akron, Ohio, the entirety of the system-oriented mental health network, as defined by the decision rules employed by Provan and Milward (1995), had organized itself into an early-stage purpose-oriented network where the state of Ohio mandated membership to a self-actualized network (see Section 5) if a provider organization wanted access to funds and clients. The idea was to integrate services through a purpose-oriented network of provider agencies convened by the state to coordinate referrals, case management, and joint programs. In the two other sites, Albuquerque, New Mexico, and Tucson, Arizona, the system-oriented network remained more loosely knit together, with conflict and competition among provider organizations and a limited degree of network governance.[8] In Albuquerque, there was a coordinating body, but it had limited authority as various state agencies contracted directly with providers. In Tucson, there was a state-funded case management agency and a state-funded core-funding agency that left a gap between funding and case management. As this study illustrates, other classes of network are often identified as nested within a study of a system-oriented

---

[8] The failure of the system in Tucson's case occurred in 1995 and led to the development of a network administrative organization (Milward & Provan, 1998; Milward & Provan, 2000) to run a purpose-oriented network for over twenty years.

network. However, the fact that the networks in all sites in this study were conceived of and constructed based on decision rules in relation to understanding mental health service provision, it is a classic example of a comparative study of system-oriented networks.

Ecology of Games Networks as System-Oriented Networks

Another body of literature that generally falls under the class of system-oriented networks is scholarship on ecology of games which is anchored in Mark Lubell's (2013) "Governing Institutional Complexity: The Ecology of Games Framework." Lubell uses an ecology of games (Long, 1958) theoretical frame to study the governance of institutional complexity in dense, highly complex policy domains. His article begins with water policy in San Francisco Bay, California. Using it as an example, Lubell documents five major collaborative institutions (as well as numerous minor ones) " . . . where stakeholders make water policy decisions" (Lubell, 2013, p. 537). All told, he identified over 100 different policy institutions operating simultaneously (Lubell et al., 2011) that govern a variety of policy issues that influence hundreds of policy actors. Without a theoretical frame, complexity of this nature would be impossible to untangle or make sense of it. Lubell uses Long's "Local Community as an Ecology of Games" (1958) as the means of bringing order to chaos.

> The core insight of . . . this framework is that governance involves multiple policy games. . . . operating simultaneously within a geographically defined policy arena, where a policy game consists of a set of policy actors participating in a rule-governed collective decisionmaking process called a "policy institution." The policy institutions that exist at a particular time and place combine to define the institutional arrangements of governance. (Lubell, 2013, p. 538)

What Lubell and colleagues have done is to take a verbal theory (Long, 1958) that has very astute insights about the interconnectedness of governance in a city like Chicago and apply them to a hugely complex and interconnected policy domain like water policy in San Francisco Bay. The ecology of games provides the sociological overlay that allows for research on multiple policy institutions governing a variety of policies related to water in one place at the same time. Rather than focusing on one policy issue or program, the ecology of games seeks to understand the impact of a particular policy on many others, hence, one game impacts many others and vice versa. The ecology of games is a portmanteau theory that fits many other frameworks, theories, and methods into its commodious confines. This includes theories of political power like pluralism and subsystem politics. Ecology of games also embraces more recent theories such as the Institutional Analysis and Development Framework of E. Ostrom (2011), the Advocacy Coalition Framework (ACF) of Paul Sabatier (1987), political games (Scharpf, 1997), and complex adaptive systems theory. Like Norton Long's "city," the games are rooted in place, be it San Francisco Bay or a Florida watershed.

Advocacy Coalitions as System-Oriented Networks

By its name, the ACF announces that it is a synthetic creation born of the work of Paul Sabbatier, Hank Jenkins Smith, Chris Weible, and many others. Actors and institutions abound in the ACF and there are coalitions within subsystems that revolve around an element of public policy. As such and similar to Ecology of Games, ACF offers a theoretical lens and associated decision rules for conceptualizing system-oriented networks. In the thirty years of its existence, it has become one of the most utilized frameworks for studying the policy process (Jenkins-Smith et al., 2014, p. 188). Network research has been used under the mantle of the ACF as an element to understanding aspects of it like a belief system among policy actors (Henry et al., 2011) or a policy subsystem as a network comprising part of a much larger nested system. Using air pollution policy in the United States, Zafonte and Sabatier (1998) used network analysis to study the behavior of advocacy coalitions. Henry, Lubell and McCoy (2011) conducted studies of networks in transportation policy. Network analysis within the tradition of the ACF is most compatible with research on policy subsystems, the primary unit of analysis for understanding public policy according to the ACF (Jenkins-Smith et al., 2014, p. 189). As we learned in Section 2, policy subsystems are equivalent to policy networks. As a framework, the ACF, like the Ecology of Games can accommodate a variety of methods, units of analysis, variables, and policy areas (called policy topics in the ACF).

Policy Networks as System-Oriented Networks

Any network that is a product of public law and thus connected to the political system of a state is a policy network.[9] These networks also fit the definition of system-oriented networks because relevant actors are delineated from nonrelevant actors by an analyst on the basis of decision rules. In political science, this comes out of the pluralist tradition of policy subsystems. Within this realm,

---

[9] Public policy is thick on the ground in advanced industrial democracies. However, new or undiscovered issues can sometimes arise quickly and become the subject of public law as child abuse did in the 1950s and 1960s in the United States (Nelson, 1984). This study illustrates the role of a precursor of policy networks, policy communities, in advancing legislation prior to its passage. With the passage of a law, the policy community becomes a policy network.

there are two main categories, " … policy implementation networks that arrange for the supply and delivery of health services through networks of organizations, and policy formation networks that both create the demand for and develop health policy" (Joosse & Milward, 2017, p. 1). Other than health policy, scholars have studied policy networks in environmental policy (Berardo, 2014), education policy (Meier & O'Toole, 2001), and transportation policy (Henry et al., 2011). All of these studies are system-oriented networks as the researcher decides which individuals, organizations, and institutions to include. Public management researchers have primarily focused on policy implementation networks; however, Laumann and Knoke (1987) analyzed policy formulation using social network analysis of the health and energy domains in the United States at the federal level, a massive study that has not been replicated. Studies of mental health policy networks in several US cities is a much less formidable task for social network methods than using it to study mental health policy formulation at the federal level. "The smaller the network examined, the more plausible SNA (social network analysis) methods become" (Joosse & Milward, 2017, p. 6). Much of the original research on policy networks focused on policy coordination and service integration across policy areas and governmental levels, a classic concern of policy implementation. Over time, other questions came to dominate the research agenda such as governance and performance. When networks supported with taxpayer dollars are governed by third parties like nonprofits or for-profit firms, how are these networks accountable to the public? How can an increasingly hollow state (Milward & Provan, 2000) hold networks accountable?

Disaster Response Networks as System-Oriented Networks

For many years, disaster response has been recognized as an inherently networked phenomenon that requires the rapid engagement and coordination of numerous organizations, agencies, and groups around a range of operational areas such as evacuations, sheltering and mass care, road closures, debris removal, utility restoration, and public safety (Drabek, 1983; Comfort, 2007; Nowell et al., 2018). While overarching governance frameworks, such as the incident command systems and the National Response Plan Emergency Support Function Framework, are suggestive of the type of unifying governance one might associate with a purpose-oriented network, studies of disaster response networks are most commonly studies of system-oriented networks. In other words, most studies of disaster response networks use analyst-imposed decision rules to delineate the network.

For example, Drabek (1983) carried out one of the earliest investigations of disaster response networks that sought to describe the network of actors associated with search and rescue operations across seven case studies. He used a snowball-sampling technique during interviews to identify relevant organizations. Comfort's (2007) longitudinal study of responders during Hurricane Katrina used data extracted from a local newspaper to identify organizations involved over time in the response phase of the hurricane. Similarly, Kapucu (2006) compiled a data set from *New York Times* reports to identify organizations engaged in response efforts during 9/11. Nowell et al.'s (2018) study of wildfire response networks was operationalized based on a predefined roster of "usual suspect" network actors based on previous fieldwork and then augmented based on nominations made during interviews. In all of these examples, the analyst defined and bounded the "network" under investigation based on a series of theoretically justified decision rules. There was no requirement that members of these disaster response networks identify that they are part of a network in order for them to be included. In fact, failure to engage effectively within the network is often a key diagnostic in response failure.

Governance Networks as System-Oriented Networks

Governance network research is associated with three different traditions in public management and policy. While all share a concern with "steering," their roots are elsewhere. Sørenson and Torfing (2005) and Torfing (2012) are rooted in the tradition of Nordic corporatism (Schmitter, 1974) coupled with postmodernist theories of discourse (Foucault, 1991; Derrida, 1992; Dryzek, 2000). Their definition of governance networks is broad and includes (1) a relatively stable horizontal articulation of interdependent, but operationally *autonomous* actors; (2) who interact through *negotiations* that involve bargaining, deliberation, and intense power struggles; (3) which take place within a *relatively institutionalized framework* of contingently articulated rules, norms, knowledge, and social imaginaries; (4) that is *self-regulating* within limits set by external agencies; and (5) which contribute to the production of *public purpose* in the broad sense of visions, ideas, plans, and regulations (Sørenson & Torfing, 2005). Networks as structures do not appear in this tradition and while they use the term "governance network," the emphasis is more on the process of governance than the structure of networks. This focus on process creates the bases for a set of decision rules that define the network within this tradition.

The "Dutch School" of governance networks is associated with Erasmus University primarily and with Kickert, Klijn, and Koppenjan (1997); Klijn and

Koppenjan (2016). The Dutch and Nordic traditions share a concern with steering and focus on government's role in steering networks. The intellectual roots of the Dutch School are in Giddens' structuration theory (1976, 1984), which is a late modernist social theory. Governance networks, in this tradition, are "used to describe public policy making and implementation through a web of relationships between government, business, and civil society actors. Governance networks are based on interdependencies, which are not necessarily equitable, between public, private and civil society actors" (Klijn, 2008, p. 511).

The third tradition of studying governance networks is rooted in the United States, Koliba, Meek, Zia, and Mills (2018) define governance networks as: "... relatively stable patterns of coordinated action and resource exchanges involving policy actors crossing different social scales, drawn from the public, private, or nonprofit sectors and across geographic levels, who interact through a variety of competitive, command and control, cooperative, and negotiated arrangements for purposes anchored in one or more facets of the policy stream." (Koliba et al., 2018 p. 260)

This tradition aligns with the European perspective but has a stronger emphasis on localized systems, application of complexity theory, and theories of democratic accountability.

It is important to note that in all three traditions, governance networks are conceptualized as the *structural manifestations of specific governance processes*. Differences among these traditions primarily reflect variations in the focal processes of interest. Because relevant network actors are defined on the basis of their engagement in these processes, different sets of decision rules for delineating network actors can be justified using different traditions. The same holds true for the related literature on collaborative governance (e.g., Ansell & Gash, 2008; Emerson et al., 2012; Keast, 2016), which has sought to delineate collaboration as a higher-order interaction relative to processes such as task integration and information sharing (Keast, 2016).

Cautionary Notes: Boundary Specification of System-Oriented Networks

Comparing apples to apples in scholarship on system-oriented networks is particularly fraught given the centrality of the network analyst in defining and delineating that which is the network from that which is not, which in turn, influences the outcomes one might observe. The delineation of networks becomes even more challenging in traditions where analysts attempt to delineate networks on the basis of some interactive process of interest. For example, if a group of actors engages in collaboration one month but then shifts to focus on task integration and coordination the next month, are these existentially two different networks? Perhaps the remedy is one proposed by Simon (1946) in which the field disciplines itself to providing a more detailed description of this analytic process and becomes more self-aware and self-critical of the consequences of the decision rules employed to construct a system-oriented network.

Laumann et al. (1983) described three approaches for identifying network actors: relational, actor characteristics, and event participation (see Table 3). Each of these approaches describes a different methodology and associated decision rules for bounding a system-oriented network and deciding who/what is included or excluded from consideration. In relational approaches, system-oriented networks are identified through snowball sampling strategies in which an initial set of actors (generally identified through either event or actor characteristic approaches) are asked to identify other actors that they interact with in some theoretically relevant way. This could be based on questions related to a policy or problem domain such as "who do you collaborate with?" or "who do you subcontract with to deliver services?". A relational approach continues this snowball sampling until either no new actors are identified or the analyst reaches some cut point for discontinuing further search. In an actor characteristic approach, actors of a system-oriented network are identified as actors who share one or more theoretically important characteristics. Last, in the event approach, system-level actors may be identified based on having been present or active during a theoretically important event.

Often different strategies are used in combination. For example, in McAllister et al. (2014), the network of actors involved in attempting to adapt to climate change in South East Queensland, Australia, was identified based primarily on event-based strategy where actors were identified as relevant to the network based on attendance for key forums that sponsored debate and negotiation surrounding climate change planning and adaptation. The authors also used an actor characteristic approach in which additional network actors were identified in which known actors fitting the criteria were asked to identify other actors also fitting the criteria (McAllister et al., 2014). In Glisson and Hemmelgarn (1998), the network of actors in children's mental health services was identified using a relational approach based on information and referral services ties in a state-sponsored pilot program.

Nowell et al. (2018) expanded upon the Laumann et al. (1983) framework, arguing that four features of the network context should be considered when developing a strategy and associated decision rules for bounding system-oriented networks (see Table 3):

1. The relative importance of formal versus informal linkages between actors within the system;
2. The potential for isolates;
3. The potential for disconnected subgroups; and
4. The extent to which the system of interest is understood to be time-bounded.

For example, actor characteristic approaches to identifying system-oriented networks often focus on the usual suspects as perceived by an analyst who is generally positioned outside of the network. These usual suspects tend to be easily identifiable agencies and organizations with institutionalized roles in the system such as school superintendents as part of the system of public education or the public health director and pediatricians in the system for improving vaccination rates. The resulting system-oriented network, based on this strategy, may obscure the role of less easily recognized actors or informal power structures. Examples might include a local religious leader active within the school district or a charter school that competes with public schools for students.

As illustrated in the aforementioned examples, commonly used approaches to identifying system actors can unintentionally exclude actors who have significant influence in explaining system-level outcomes but whose influence within the network is informal, like the religious leader in the previous paragraph, or important actors who are isolates. Isolates and disconnected subgroups are actors within system-oriented networks who, for whatever reason, are not connected to other actors in the system on any relationship used for network identification. Often, understanding disconnected actors is a key diagnostic of interest for analysts of system-oriented networks as it helps to explain things such as operational silos. For example, following a disaster, it is not uncommon to have individuals in untraditional roles become engaged in response and relief efforts but operate in relative isolation from other responders (Simo & Bies, 2007; Nolte & Boenigk, 2011). Other examples of operational silos might include First Nations in Canada and Child and Youth Health Networks that operate in parallel but where Indigenous kids may fall through the cracks between them. By nature of their disconnectedness, it is easy to miss isolates or disconnected subgroups using relational snowball sampling approaches for understanding system-oriented networks.

Finally, if an analyst is interested in a system-oriented network that endures and supersedes beyond the boundaries of a given event that brings actors or a portion of actors together – event-based approaches for identifying system-oriented networks carry the risk of under-representing key actors. For example, if one wishes to understand disaster response networks as system-oriented networks that supersede any one disaster – an event-based approach associated with a specific disaster may offer too narrow of a view and fail to consider key actors. Other examples might include efforts to understand modern social movements that often emerge out of networks established during preceding movements. For example, if a scholar defines the system-oriented network based on attendance at a contemporary rally or organizing event, they may miss the historical networks that preceded and helped to shape the current network structure and character. Table 3 offers guidance for assisting the system-oriented network analyst in designing decision rules and appropriate protocols for identifying the actors within a system-oriented network based on considerations of the relevant characteristics of that context.

Summary and Conclusion

System-oriented networks are networks conceptualized by a network analyst to represent the population of actors, and their interactions, germane to some system of interest, generally associated with a policy, program, or problem domain. The unique feature of the system-oriented network is that it is defined and brought into being by a network analyst who conceives of the network – based on a set of decision rules justified based on their theoretical importance for understanding some systemic outcome of interest.

In this way, scholarship on system-oriented networks is linked to the traditions and methodologies associated with social science perspectives on systems. To understand the former, one must have some grounding in the latter. Systems thinking includes a preoccupation with ideas such as relationships between parts and wholes, feedback loops, processes of emergence, hierarchical nesting of systems, and holism. In the social sciences, an epistemological perspective that sees systems as a heuristic defined by the analyst's preconceptions and interests dominates systems thinking. However, the way in which the system is formulated ought to be grounded in empirical referents. In public management and policy, we frequently speak of systems (the welfare system, the justice system, the education system, the healthcare system) as real entities, just as we speak of system-oriented networks as real entities. However, at their core, both systems and system-oriented networks are abstractions. In the system-oriented class of network scholarship, the network is thus a property of a larger preconceived system defined by the analyst. We have identified the following types of system-oriented networks, although the list is by no means exclusive:

1. A **Service Implementation Network** is one where the payer, most often the government, picks the players. The players are those agencies who become

Table 3 Key consideration when determining a network bounding approach for system–oriented networks*

Network feature important to research context	Description	Cues to aid in the determination of a bounding approach	Recommended bounding approach		
			Relational	Positional or reputational actor characteristics	Event participation
Institutional norms and structures	Informal or formal rules and processes that emerge as patterns because they are ingrained in the fabric of the network and ties among actors	Does the research question (RQ) have a primary focus on *informal* ties between actors or informal *power* structures?	✓		
		Does the RQ focus on understanding formal ties and processes among actors?		✓	
Isolates	Actors who have no direct relational ties	Does the RQ address questions related to the presence of *all* actors important to the domain, regardless of their connections to others?		✓	✓
Disconnected subgroups	Cliques or factions within the network that do not share relational ties with other parts of the network	Does the RQ seek to identify the existence or roles of cliques or factions within the network that do not share relational ties with other parts of the network?		✓	✓
History and duration	Permanence of ties between actors over time	Does the RQ explore a network characterized by enduring relationships over time? Are the historical roots of the network important?	✓	✓	

* Adapted from Nowell et al. (2018).

contractors for the funder. Service implementation networks vary greatly in the degree to which they are integrated. This can vary from a series of one-off "make or buy" decisions by an agency to a well-integrated network of service providers.

2. A body of literature that falls under the class of system-oriented networks is called an "**Ecology of Games**," which is a governance framework involving multiple policy games, operating simultaneously within a geographically defined policy arena. The policy institutions that exist at a particular time and place combine to define the institutional arrangements of governance.

3. The **ACF** consists of a multitude of actors and institutions within subsystems and there are coalitions within the subsystems that revolve around an element of public policy. Similar to Ecology of Games, ACF offers a theoretical lens and associated decision rules for conceptualizing system-oriented networks.

4. A **Policy Network** is any network that is a product of public law and thus connected to the political system of a state. These networks fit the definition of system-oriented networks because an analyst creates decision rules that delineate relevant actors from nonrelevant actors. Much of the original research on policy networks focused on policy coordination and service integration across policy areas and governmental levels, a classic concern of policy implementation.

5. **Disaster Response Networks** are defined and bounded by the analyst, typically using the scope of the disaster and the organizations and institutions that responded to it. There is no requirement that members of these disaster response networks identify that they are part of a network in order for them to be included. In fact, failure to engage effectively within the network is often a key diagnostic in response failure.

6. **Governance Networks** are associated with three different traditions in public management and policy. All share a concern with "steering." There is the tradition of Nordic corporatism coupled with postmodernist theories of discourse. Networks as nodes and edges do not appear and the emphasis is more on the process of governance. The Dutch tradition shares a concern with the government's role in steering networks with the Nordic tradition. The third tradition of studying governance networks is rooted in the United States. While the US tradition aligns somewhat with the Nordic and Dutch traditions, it has a stronger emphasis on localized systems, application of complexity theory, and theories of democratic accountability.

5 Purpose-Oriented Networks

With the passage of the Violence Against Women Act (VAWA) in 1994, provisions were made for federal grants that would be awarded to local communities toward the creation of a comprehensive and coordinated response to domestic violence. The conditions of this grant mandated formal collaboration between the local court system, law enforcement, and domestic violence service providers. These funds led to the formation of domestic violence coordinating councils (DVCCs) across the United States. One such example is the Harris County Domestic Violence Coordinating Council (www.hcdvcc.org) located in Houston, TX. This DVCC was convened in 1996 by the county district attorney and the Houston police chief who brought together community leaders and stakeholders from across the county to "address victim safety, batterer accountability and prevention" [www.hcdvcc.org/about/history/]. The Harnett County DVCC has been working together ever since and is an example of our third, and final, class of network studied within public management and policy: purpose-oriented networks. **The taxonomic definition of this class of network is bounded, self-referencing collectives comprised of actors who consciously affiliate to the collective around some shared purpose.** In this section, we describe the characteristics of this taxonomic class, provide examples, and offer justification for the theoretical importance of these characteristics as demarcations of the class from system-oriented and structural-oriented networks.

Carboni et al. (2019)[10] described a purpose-oriented network as "a network comprised of three or more autonomous actors who participate in a joint effort based on a common purpose" (p. 210). In their analysis, they argue that purpose, membership, joint effort, and governance are four constituent dimensions of purpose-oriented networks. We build upon this definition in an effort to delineate purpose-oriented networks from their taxonomic counterparts: system-oriented and structural-oriented networks. Indeed, as discussed at greater length in Section 4, system-oriented networks can also be comprised of actors sharing a common purpose who engage with one another in joint efforts in accordance with institutionalized rules. If multiple classes of networks can be comprised of actors who affiliated within a common problem area, what is it that makes purpose-oriented unique as a separate class of network?

We argue purpose-oriented networks are delineated from other network classes by virtue of the fact that they have self-actualized as an entity. To actualize means to make actual or real, to realize, or to become actual (*Merriam Webster*). To self-actualize is, therefore, the act of realizing oneself or making

---

[10] See also *Perspectives of Public Management and Governance* 2019, Special Issue on Purpose-Oriented Networks, Vol 2, Issue 3.

oneself real or actual. The term became popularized by Maslow in his model of human motivation in which he refers to self-actualization as the realization of one's full potential (Maslow, 1967). However, for our purposes, we use the term network self-actualization simply to refer to networks that have collectively formed a clear sense of identity as an entity. We draw from decades of sociological, organizational, and social-psychological research and theory to argue that networks that have self-actualized as an entity are a fundamentally different social phenomenon relative to other network classes. As with the other two classes, theories and scholarship within this class of networks cannot be assumed to translate to other classes without careful attention to what makes purpose-oriented networks unique.

Network Self-Actualization

We argue that a network becomes purpose-oriented, achieving self-actualization through the achievement of three conditions: It becomes (1) self-referencing, (2) has a bounded membership, and (3) its members consciously affiliate in relation to some shared purpose (Figure 5). Next, we describe each of these criteria in more detail.

Self-referencing: The first criterion for a purpose-oriented network is that it must be self-referencing, which occurs when a network refers to itself as a collective entity.[11] For example, a purpose-oriented network will generally name itself (e.g., the Partnership for a Healthy Durham; the Hiwassee River Watershed Coalition). Further acts of self-reference include a network creating products or artifacts such as setting up a website or publication that refers to the

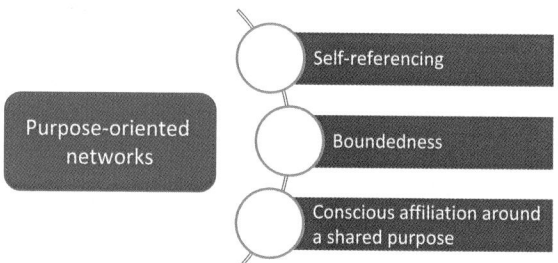

Figure 5 Network self-actualization
This figure shows the three conditions that must be achieved for a network to achieve self-actualization.

---

[11] We plead guilty to reification. A network becomes self-referencing when its members refer to it by name in conversation and written documents. Some self-referencing networks have "terms of reference" that explicitly name the network and specify what obligations the members have to the network.

network as an entity. Self-reference is a critical step for a network in the formation of a collective identity and for facilitating member identification with the network. Scholars have long recognized social categorization and group identity formation as powerful forces in shaping human societies. When a network of actors engages in self-reference, it is seeking to establish the basis for a group identity. We know group identity is a crucial element for facilitating collective action as it facilitates the creation of group attributes, norms, and shared purpose that engender loyalty and commitment to the group and a willingness to act on behalf of the group (Brewer & Silver, 2000). The stronger the collective identity within the network, the more members will be disposed to trust other members of the network and take action on behalf of, and in the interests of, the network (Frank, 2009). This process is particularly important in light of well-documented tensions common to purpose-oriented networks in reconciling the diversity of interests into a coherent path forward (Saz-Carranza & Ospina, 2011) and the "two-hat problem" (Milward et al., 2016) of networks in which individuals acting as representatives of organizations or agencies can experience role conflict between their loyalty to the network and to their organization. The development of trust and norms of reciprocity are key for collaborative governance (Axelrod, 1984 Gray & Purdy, 2018). In this way, a collective identity becomes an invaluable resource a network can leverage in pursuit of shared aims.

Boundedness: The second criterion for purpose-oriented networks is bounded membership. By this, we mean that members of purpose-oriented networks are able to identify one another and distinguish members from nonmembers. The theoretical importance of bounded membership also links back to considerable social-psychological research, particularly that of social categorization theory (Turner, 2010), which argues that evolution drives humans to form social groups that optimize the competing needs for distinctiveness and belonging (Brewer & Silver, 2000). As such, humans will develop stronger identification with groups that have clear boundaries. In addition, clear group boundaries facilitate the development of group norms which further increases both group identification and trust in-group members (Kramer et al., 1996). As stated by Brewer and Silver (2000):

> In order to engage member identification and loyalty, groups must have explicit, agreed upon rules of inclusion and exclusion that define clear boundaries between in group and out group. Effective groups must have defined criteria for group membership that meet the needs for secure inclusion and belonging. (p. 155)

They further argue, **given that "indiscriminate trust and indiscriminate distrust are costly," it is important for group boundaries to be recognized by all parties in order to delineate the limits of risk** (Brewer & Silver, 2000). This sentiment on the importance of group boundaries has been echoed by scholars of purpose-oriented networks. For example, Gray and Purdy (2018) argue "from the onset, agreements need to be reached about who has a legitimate right to participate in the partnership . . .". Emerson and Nabatchi (2015) discuss the importance of decision-making concerning who should be included at the table in CGRs. Bryson, Crosby, and Stone (2006) noted formal descriptions of members as an element of formal agreement that set the stage for the work of a cross-sector collaboration.

Purpose-oriented networks will vary in the level of boundedness, with some networks welcoming almost anyone who expresses an interest to join while other networks will be closed to only a predetermined set of actors or have more stringent requirements for gaining membership. Purpose-oriented networks may even have different criteria for different members. For example, the Community Partnership of Southern Arizona community mental health network had different levels of financial commitment for those agencies whose CEO's sat on their board than for agencies that did not. However, all purpose-oriented networks will have some collectively recognized mechanism for identifying who are members and distinguishing them from nonmembers, even if this is just a membership list.

Conscious affiliation around a shared purpose: The last criterion for assignment of a network into the class of purpose-oriented networks is the requirement that members of a purpose-oriented network consciously affiliate to the network around a shared purpose. In a review of the network literature in public administration, Isett et al. (2011) posed the question whether network actors " . . . must acknowledge and accept that they operate in a network for it to actually be a network?" (p. 2). While it is not true for the other classes, for purpose-oriented networks the answer to this question is, unequivocally, *yes*. Further, members must not only acknowledge, but **consciously affiliate** to the network around a shared purpose. In other words, there must be some degree of awareness and social identification for there to be a purpose-oriented network. It is noteworthy that in order to consciously affiliate to a network around a shared purpose, a network must be recognized to exist (be self-referencing) and the network's general reason for existing must be broadly understood among all the members. This does not suggest that members will not have their own unique portfolio of interests which motivates them to affiliate to a purpose-oriented network that extends beyond its purpose. This will undoubtedly be the case. It also does not require that network members necessarily agree on the specific goals of a network as goals may be negotiated and renegotiated over time (Gray & Purdy, 2018). **The criterion of conscious affiliation around a shared purpose only requires that there is some shared purpose that is recognized by *all* members as *the reason that the network exists*.** If an actor can be conceived of as part of a network but not necessarily know it, it is a clear indication that the network in question is not a purpose-oriented network.

The Unique Capabilities of Purpose-Oriented Networks

When networks emerge or are created that are self-referencing and have a bounded membership that consciously affiliates around a shared purpose, they are a self-actualized, purpose-oriented network. Purpose-oriented networks have emerged as commonplace phenomenon in numerous policy domains. Another example is the Valley Stewardship Network (VSN). The VSN is a purpose-oriented network.   It self-identifies (self-reference) as a "network of collaborative conversation-minded organizations" associated with the Kickapoo and neighboring watersheds in Southwestern Wisconsin. The membership of the VSN consists of nineteen partner organizations (bounded membership) that consciously affiliate with the VSN for in order to "share experience, best practices, and new ideas for the protection of land and water" and offer " . . . assistance and access to the many programs available to support good stewardship by farmers, landowners, and all who enjoy our area" (conscious affiliation around a shared purpose; retrieved on October 15, 2022from https://valleystewardshipnetwork.org/about-us/our-partners/).

We argue that self-actualized entities like the VSN are fundamentally different from the other two network classes. Specifically, we argue that the three defining characteristics of self-reference, bounded membership, and conscious affiliation around a shared purpose create the opportunity for a whole range of

Table 4 Delineating characteristics of purpose-oriented networksNetwork is self-referencing; it has given itself a name and/or has created artifacts (e.g., reports, web pages) in which it refers to itself as an entity.

➢ Network membership is bounded such that members are able to identify other members and distinguish them from nonmembers.
➢ Network members consciously affiliate with the network.
➢ There is a recognized purpose understood by all members as the reason that the network exists.

collective capabilities that are not possible in the absence of these three conditions. This is not to say these capabilities are definitional to being a purpose-oriented network. A network only needs to be self-actualized to be a purpose-oriented network. Rather, it is to say that *only* purpose-oriented networks like the VSN *are able* to have these capabilities. Here, we discuss three examples of the unique capabilities of purpose-oriented networks: (1) the formation of network-level goals, (2) the creation of an overarching system of governance, and (3) network agency and representation within the broader environment.

Formation and evaluation of network-level goals: The concept of network-level goals is problematic in networks that are not self-referencing and where membership and conscious affiliation are uncertain. For a goal to be ascribed to a network, this suggests the network, as an entity consisting of its members, affirms the legitimacy of the goal and that the goal is the property or character-istic of the network. If a network is not self-actualized as an entity, it is hard to envision how members might legitimate a goal as reflecting a network-level aspiration. This is not to suggest that goals do not motivate behavior in other network classes. Rather, we argue that these goals are likely the attributes of actors within the network and thus cannot be construed to reflect a network-level attribute unless it is viewed as an emergent, aggregate, property reflecting the collection of goals associated with different network actors. In other words, when working in networks that are not self-actualized, discussions of goals must be accompanied by clarification concerning, whose goal is it? In contrast, purpose-oriented networks, by nature of being self-actualized as an entity, are able to set goals that are legitimated by the members as reflecting the goals of the network although individual adherence to the goals may vary among the members. For example, the Arizona Coalition of Military Families has a goal of "functional zero" for homeless veterans.

Overarching network governance systems: The concepts of network and collaborative governance has received considerable attention in the literature (e.g., Ansell & Gash, 2008; Provan & Kenis, 2008; Emerson & Nabatchi, 2015; Koliba et al., 2018). We argue that considerations of governance can be relevant in any class of network; however, it is likely to look and operate under different authority within our three different classes.[12] Some authors have theorized

---

[12] While some network scholars might argue that structural-oriented networks lack a conscious governance activity by actors, rational choice institutionalism, historical institutionalism, and cultural institutionalism all acknowledge that norms develop in social systems which govern/ constrain behavior – for example, some early sociological network studies of diamond traders in NYC (Richman, 2006).

about intentionally designed, and collectively agreed upon, governance systems in which there is a single mode of governance that applies to the network as a whole (e.g., Provan & Kenis, 2008). We suggest these theories are likely most applicable in purpose-oriented networks. For example, Provan and Kenis (2008) describe three modes of network governance: member-led, lead organization, and network administrative organizations. These modes of governance raise interesting questions about the nature of authority and consent of the governed within networks. Network administrative organizations (NAOs) are a superordinate organization whose members either acquiesce or grant authority to an administrative entity to govern the network.[13] There is variance in the administrative capacity of NAOs, some have been granted authority to fully govern the network while others have more limited administrative functions like accounting, contracting, and personnel, leaving governance elsewhere (Milward & Provan, 1998).

While NAOs may vary in the scope of their authority to govern a network, they all must have some basis of authority to represent the network as an entity. A purpose-oriented network, as a self-actualized entity, is able to set goals and delegate authority to an NAO to support the network in accomplishing those goals. Delegation of authority is more conceptually problematic at a network level in other classes of networks as the network is not self-actualized as a singular entity and therefore cannot collectively grant authority. Indeed, different actors may seek to govern different parts of the network, potentially toward different ends (Rethemyer & Hatmaker, 2008). This is not to say that networks in other classes do not have institutionalized rules, interdependencies, and power relationships which can lead to predictable patterns of behavior within the network (North, 1990). But, this is different from an overarching governance system that has been designed, and consented to, by its members such as the modes of network governance as described by authors such as Provan and Kenis (2008). This ability to intentionally create a governance system and gain the consent or acquiescence of the governed is a unique capability of purpose-oriented networks.

Collective action and representation within the broader environment: Perhaps one of the most profound capabilities unique to purpose-oriented networks is the ability of the network to take purposeful, strategic collective action and be recognized as a legitimate entity within the broader environment (Human &

---

[13] The NAO's authority may be granted by a state or local government that will only contract with the NAO for a set of community services. Its authority may come from the member organizations in the network who grant the NAO the authority to act in the name of the network. Creating an NAO may also be a requirement of a philanthropic funder.

Provan, 2000; Nowell et al., 2018). As a counterfactual illustration, take the network of scholars engaged in research about networks in public management and policy. Few would disagree that this group is a network. It is comprised of a highly interconnected and interdependent collection of actors. They meet at the same conferences year after year or organize their own specialized workshops. There is a significant level of cohesion within the network. There are institutionalized rules that govern much of the behavior within the network. There is a general sense of purpose that coheres the network around the common agenda of advancing the state of knowledge about networks. However, this group of actors does not meet the criteria of a purpose-oriented network. It lacks a self-referencing identity; members refer to it in abstract, not in specific terms. There are no agreed-upon boundaries delineating the population of members. Descriptions of relevant members would likely look different depending on who you asked. Finally, membership in this network is defined by decision rules and not conscious consent. A highly cited author would likely be considered part of the network regardless of whether they wanted anything to do with us or not.

Because this network is not self-actualized as an entity, it cannot act as an entity nor can it be represented as an entity within the broader environment. To illustrate this, imagine the eyebrow raising that would occur within our example network if a network member – even a highly central one – were to stand up in front of a national conference and proclaim that they were speaking on behalf of the scholars who study networks in public management and policy. No actor – regardless of how central to the network – can be granted authority to speak or act on behalf of the network because the network has not self-actualized into an entity capable of granting that authority. Networks are able to set goals, develop strategies, and take action as a collective only once their members have established the governance structures that allow for organization to occur and for members to consent, or at least acquiesce, to be represented (Gray & Purdy, 2018). Again, this is not to say that collective action does not occur within networks of other classes. It certainly does. However, it arises at a different level of analysis, generally occurring within dyads and subgroups or as an emergent property of a network based on the summation of dyadic and subgroup organizing.

Apples to Apples: The Study of Purpose-Oriented Networks in Public Management and Policy

Purpose-oriented networks have become commonplace as institutionalized best practice for confronting complex public issues (e.g., Chapman & Varda, 2017;

Nowell & Kenis, 2019). Although they have been referred to by different names (Lemaire et al., 2019), the public management and policy literature has a long and rich history of theorizing and investigating purpose-oriented networks. Prominent efforts include Bryson et al.'s (2006, 2015) model of cross-sector collaborations; work on CGRs (Emerson et al., 2012; Emerson & Nabatchi, 2015), the public management literature on goal-directed networks (e.g., Saz-Carranza & Ospina, 2011; Lemaire & Provan, 2012; Raab et al., 2015), work on goal-oriented advocacy networks (Saz-Carranza, 2012), and Agranoff's (2007) work on public management networks. This list is far from comprehensive and is only intended to illustrate the breadth of scholarship dedicated to the study of purpose-oriented networks and the associated diversity of labels embraced within this literature. Each of these scholars has a distinctive theoretical and contextual focus as illustrated by the proposed frameworks, the diversity of cases selected, and conditions for case inclusion. For example, Agranoff (2007) focuses specifically on networks involving multiple government actors. Emerson and Nabatchi (Emerson et al., 2012; Emerson & Nabatchi, 2015) are particularly interested in networks in which there is significant perception of competing interests among participants but where the representatives of those interests have made a commitment to principled engagement in pursuit of collaborative decision-making. Saz-Carranza (2012) focuses on advocacy networks governed by NAOs in the immigration domain. While all meet our criteria for purpose-oriented networks, there is rich and theoretically meaningful diversity among different types of purpose-oriented networks. However, here, we focus explicitly on what these diverse streams of literature have in common to justify their consideration as a taxonomic class we call purpose-oriented networks.

Cross-sector partnerships as purpose-oriented networks: One of the more influential works in the field was an article on the design and implementation of what was termed cross-sector collaborations or partnerships written by Bryson, Crosby, and Stone in 2006 and later revisited in 2015. In the original article, Bryson et al. (2006) described cross-sector collaborations as "the linking or sharing of information, resources, activities, and capabilities by organizations in two or more sectors to achieve jointly an outcome that could not be achieved by organizations in one sector separately" (p. 44). This definition, alone, focuses primarily on composition of the network and could be used to describe any of the three classes. For example, in an agency's ego network, the agency may partner with different nongovernmental organizations to achieve some outcome that would not have otherwise been possible. Alternatively, many system-oriented networks are comprised of actors representing different sectors, connected through a web of various ties involving information sharing and collaboration among different actors. However, the framework proposed by Bryson et al. (2006) indicates their theoretical focus was not on structural- or system-oriented networks. They discuss members of the cross-sector partnerships being drawn from an institutionalized environment comprised of a web of existing relationships or networks. In other words, they describe cross-sector partnerships forming out of structural- and system-oriented networks. They recount the role of conveners, or brokering organizations, who facilitated the formation of the collaboration, suggesting cross-sector collaborations were purposefully convened and, thus, self-referencing entities. Perhaps most illuminating, and our justification for including their framework in this class, is their argument that agreement on a broadly shared purpose, designation of formal leadership, and articulation of membership as key formative characteristics of the partnership that will set the stage for later outcomes (Bryson et al., 2006). Finally, the authors speak at length about network-level outcomes such as "survival," "effectiveness," and the importance of accountability systems to track inputs, processes, and outcomes at a network level. These outcome-oriented descriptors offer relatively clear evidence that their influential framework assumes self-referencing, bounded entity comprised of members who have purposefully convened around a shared purpose.[14]

Collaborative governance regimes as purpose-oriented networks: CGRs introduced by Emerson and Nabatchi in 2012 and further explicated in their 2015 book, are defined as a "particular mode of, or system for, public decision making in which cross boundary collaboration represents the prevailing pattern of behavior and activity" (Emerson et al., 2012, p. 6). This definition embraces a process-focused lens on modes of cross-boundary institutional collaboration. The authors argue that this mode of "cross boundary institutional cooperation" (p. 19) will stabilize in such a manner as to represent an institutionalized entity. While some have argued that CGR's and purpose-oriented networks are different, in an email exchange with Emerson (2020) she states that "I have been saying for some time that CGRs and public purpose oriented networks are indeed studying similar phenomena, but through different conceptual and methodological lens, not just assumptions about human nature."[15] There are several cues to suggest that CGRs, as conceptualized by Emerson and Nabatchi (2015) fit into the class of purpose-oriented networks. First, like cross-sector

---

[14] It is noteworthy that purpose-oriented networks are not the focus of Bryson and Crosby's (1992, 2005) equally influential book *Leadership for the Common Good.* We include this book in Section 2 on The Intellectual Development of Three Disciplinary Lenses on Networks.

[15] Email exchange between Kirk Emerson and H. Brinton Milward, December 28, 2020.

partnerships, CGRs are described as an entity that is intentionally "formed" (p. 27) or "initiated" (p. 28), and comprised of participants organized around a collective purpose, suggesting a self-referencing entity comprised of consciously affiliating members rather than the manifested entities that are the consequence of polycentricity in some larger system of interest. The criteria of conscious affiliation and self-reference are further reinforced by their assumption of principled engagement of participants as a core collaborative process and in their description of decision-making processes that usually involve "working toward some form of consensus, that all participants either agree or can live with" (p. 33). Finally, Emerson and Nabatchi (2015) describe decisions about who gets to participate is a key consideration for CGRs indicating there is a clear boundary to CGRs that allows them to distinguish members from nonmembers and exclude undesirable or uncooperative members.

Goal-directed/whole networks as purpose-oriented networks: Another growing body of literature on purpose-oriented networks has taken place under the heading of goal-directed or whole networks (e.g., Raab & Kenis, 2009; Saz-Carranza & Ospina, 2011; Iborra et al., 2018; Lemaire, 2020). This literature commonly references back to definitions provided by Provan, Fish, and Sydow (2007), as well as Provan and Kenis (2008), describing goal-directed networks as "groups of three or more legally autonomous organizations that work together to achieve not only their own goals but also a collective goal" (Provan & Kenis, 2008, p. 231). Examples of networks represented in this literature include an immigration advocacy network that was given the pseudonym of the West Network by Saz-Carranza and Ospina (2011). In their case description, the authors state, "[i]n 1995, different progressive nonprofits joined to create West Network and to defeat anti-immigrant ballot measures being prepared for circulation to voters of a west coast state" (p. 338). This network consisted of sixteen members, governed by a board of directors, and operating under a mission statement that read, "[t]o promote immigrant rights and well-being and to counter the growing anti-immigrant agenda in Oregon." (p. 339). Another example is the Southern Alberta Child and Youth Health Network (SACYHN) studied by Lemaire (2020). SACYHN was a network serving Southern Alberta, Canada, comprised of primarily public organizations "voluntarily working together to better address child and youth health and well-being". Lemaire (2020) described SACYHN as governed by a steering committee and funded primarily through the Calgary Health Authority. Internet searches on this network reveal a series of artifacts including a series of health assessment reports with authorship credit attributed to SACYHN. These cases offer clear-cut examples of networks that have self-actualized as entities.

Public management networks as purpose-oriented networks: In 2007, Robert Agranoff wrote an influential book on the management of what he termed "public management networks." He defined public management networks as "collaborative structures that bring together representatives from public agencies and NGOs to address problems of common concern that accrue value to the manager/specialists, their participating organizations and their networks" (p. 2). The concept of representatives brought together around common problems is suggestive of an entity with members who consciously affiliate around a shared purpose. On the other hand, this could also refer to management of an ego network by a public agency, which was the primary focus of his earlier research (Agranoff & McGuire, 2003). However, the cases investigated and used to illustrate management principles in this Element offer clear depictions of purpose-oriented networks (Agranoff, 2007). These cases include self-referencing entities such as the "Darby Partnership," the "Indiana Economic Development Council," the "Partnership for Rural Nebraska," the "Iowa Geographic Information Council," and the "Small Communities Infrastructure Group." A closer look at these cases illustrates why we classify these case studies as purpose-oriented networks. For example, the small communities environmental infrastructure group of Ohio (www.scwie.org) is a network comprised of federal, state, and local agencies; NGOs; service providers; and education organizations to work on water and wastewater infrastructure needs for small communities in Ohio. Founded by the Ohio Water Development Authority, the network receives funding for its initiatives through a variety of federal and state funders. The members are comprised of funders, representatives from Ohio's regional planning commission, and local development districts. According to Agranoff, the network's goals are stated in a published document referred to as the "Small Communities Goals and Objectives 2002." It has a subcommittee structure that meets regularly to carry out the work of the network. One other example presented by Agranoff is the case of the Darby Partnership. The Darby Partnership (www.bigdarby.org) is a network formed to protect the Big and Little Darby Creek Watershed that spans a six-county region in Ohio. The members of this public management network began as a partnership between the six counties that are part of the Darby Creek Watershed, the Ohio EPA, and the Department of Natural Resources. Over time, additional agencies were brought into the partnership to assist with watershed improvement and management efforts. The network meets regularly to share information and offer technical assistance to members. Agranoff described this partnership as an informational network because its primary agenda is to serve as an information clearinghouse that serves to seed a number of spin-off initiatives among various members of the network (2007).

Collective impact as purpose-oriented networks: While not a product of scholarly research, in the past ten years, a new form of network has appeared in the world of practice that seems to fit the definition of a purpose-oriented network. The term "collective impact" first appeared in an article by John Kania and Mark Kramer (2011) of FSG Consulting in the *Stanford Social Innovation Review*. They define collective impact as "the commitment of a group of important actors from the different sectors to a common agenda for solving a specific social problem" (Shumate & Cooper, 2016, p. 1). After giving several examples of what they view as exemplary cross-sector collaborations, they attempt to distill the elements that made them successful. These five elements are a list of prescriptions that networks or collaborations should follow if they want to achieve "collective impact."

Common agenda: All partners share a vision for change that includes a shared understanding of and approach to the problem.

Shared measurement system: Partners commit to collect data and evaluate results using the same criteria.

Mutually reinforcing activities: Rather than create new programs, partners coordinate and align activities so that they support one another and fit into an overall plan.

Continuous communication: Collective impact calls for trust and a common vocabulary, which are built in part through frequent meetings and Web-based tools.

Backbone organization: Because coordinating collective impact efforts is time-intensive, a backbone organization is required to coordinate partners and efforts.

This model of organizing purpose-oriented networks has been adopted by a number of philanthropic funders as best practice and expect grant recipients to adopt these principles. With the exception of a few attempts to interact with network researchers (Shumate & Cooper, 2016) this endeavor remains a commercial product, albeit a popular one with United Ways and other funders.

Summary and Conclusion

Our class of purpose-oriented networks refers to networks that have evolved into self-actualized entities. This means that they have formed a collective identity as a group, have given themselves a name, and engage in self-reference. Networks in this class have bounded their membership such that members can reliably distinguish members from nonmembers. Finally, all members in purpose-oriented networks know that they are part of a network. They all consciously affiliate with the network around some shared sense of purpose, even if the goals of individual members and their aspirations for what the network will accomplish differ. This means all members can reliably provide a common narrative about the basic reason for why the network exists. Cross-sector partnerships, community collaboratives, collaborative governance regimes, whole networks, goal-directed networks, public management networks, and collective impact networks[16] generally all refer to purpose-oriented networks.

Purpose-oriented networks are unique. They are able to do things that networks in other classes cannot. Because they have self-actualized as entities that are sociologically real to their members, these networks are able to create structures and processes for establishing network-level goals and systems of governance that allow for the reconciliation of competing interests into a shared agenda. These networks can decide upon actions they will carry out as collective, they can evaluate and be evaluated to determine the efficacy of these actions in relation to their goals. Finally, the purpose-oriented network can represent its membership in interactions with other entities in its environment. This allows the many to speak as one.

It is, therefore, not surprising that the formation of purpose-oriented networks has become viewed as a best practice as a tool for addressing complex policy issues that are beyond the scope of any single organization or agency to address. Purpose-oriented networks have been shown to be powerful change agents for organizing and improving communication and coordination in institutionally complex environments. We are just starting to learn about the implications of the effectiveness of the widespread implementation of this class of networks.

---

[16] If the form of collective impact does not meet the actuality of our criteria, it may not be a purpose-oriented network.

6 The Pocket Field Guide to Classifying Networks

This taxonomy is our attempt to offer the field of public management and policy a common nomenclature and an associated set of diagnostic tools to help inform the study of networks. Our hope is that it will facilitate better conversations among scholars, practitioners, and network analysts. From better conversations comes better theory, comparative research, and management. Currently, scholars speak of "networks" in reference to very different classes of phenomena from communities of practice to disaster response networks. We want them to have a way to understand one another. At the same time, our hope is that scholars who study similar entities but who have been trained in separate traditions and use different labels will be better able to leverage the full range of theoretical lenses available for understanding their class of networks should they desire to do so – regardless of the labels they use.

As we have stated previously, we do not propose that this taxonomy replace all existing network labels or that there are no meaningful differences between network entities of the same class: Our goal is not to convince scholars to relabel their network entities of interest. Such an effort would be both futile and counterproductive. Significant literatures have evolved around many of these labels and this diversity of conceptual lenses and network entities is part of what makes this tapestry of scholarship so rich and engaging. Rather, we advocate that scholars utilize this taxonomy as a tool to help describe those entities, positioning them within the broader class of related entities so that it becomes easier to conduct comparative network research – in other words, compare apples to apples. At the same time, we hope appropriate class identification will lead to more careful comparative work across classes. In other words, help us to avoid theoretical missteps in unknowingly comparing apples to bananas.

Positioning Networks within the Appropriate Class

It is the role of the analyst, who conceives of a network as an entity, to situate their network within its respective class. However, class assignments should be empirically supported and verifiable by an independent observer. The taxonomic classes presented in this Element have the advantage of being empirically verifiable and applicable no matter what theoretical perspective or disciplinary lens an analyst wishes to privilege in understanding a network. In 1946, Herbert Simon admonished the field of public administration to improve its methods for describing and analyzing administrative situations in order to advance both theory and practice (Simon, 1946). Consistent with this advice, this taxonomy is designed to advance our methods and nomenclature for describing and theorizing about network entities in a manner that allows for the comparison of apples to apples. We propose that the most fundamental distinction that must first be established in describing network entities is whether the network of interest is a *structural-oriented network, a system-oriented network*, or *a purpose-oriented network*. **This classification speaks to the existential nature of the entity being referred to as a network**. In this section, we provide scholars with a common language and set of tools for diagnosing and describing network entities in each of these taxonomic classes.

Structural-oriented networks (to review see, Table 5) are delineated as a class by the fact that they are not presumed to represent a higher-order system or self-actualized group. A structurally oriented network has no existential identity outside of its consequences for its component parts. Structural

Table 5 Summary of taxonomic classes

Taxonomic Class	Description	Diagram	Legend
Structural-oriented network(s): **Ego-centric**	A focal actor's (or set of actors') relations with other *actors as it relates to a focal actor*		⬤ Focal Actor ⬤ Actor ▬ Edge
Structural-oriented network(s): **Dyadic**	Patterns of tie creation and deletion among a *sample of actors within an arbitrarily bounded population*		⬤ Actor ▬ Edge
System-oriented network(s)	The collection of actors associated with a system of interest and the nature of their actions and interactions		⬤ Actors ▢ Embedded Purpose-oriented networks ⬭ Theoretical boundary of the system of interest
Purpose-oriented network(s)	A bounded, self-referencing network comprised of actors who *consciously affiliate* with the network around a shared purpose or concern		⬤ Actors ▢ Purpose-oriented network

components of networks are nodes and their ties to each other. Structural-oriented networks represent the "relational turn" in the social sciences, where, beginning in the 1930s, the nature of social relations among human beings became the focus of study. From Jacob Moreno's (1934) studies of the sociometry of relationships among runaway young women emerged a rich body of literature for measuring social structure. The theoretical focus is on the components of the network – nodes or ties – and the consequences of network composition and structure for the nodes and ties. Structural-oriented networks can be further divided into ego-centric networks and dyadic networks. In an ego-centric network, the network is conceptualized as an attribute of a focal actor. It is comprised of the sum of actors and pattern of ties associated with that actor. In a dyadic network, the focus is on the nature, formation, patterning, and evolution of ties themselves.

System-oriented networks are entities conceived of by the analyst, based on a set of decision rules for determining who or what is and is not part of the network based on its relevance to one or more systems of interest, be it a mental health system or a disaster response system. They do not have a stable and agreed-upon identity outside the conception of the network analyst, as different analysts may view the network differently and employ different decision rules for inclusion or exclusion. In contrast, **purpose-oriented networks** are entities that have self-actualized, meaning they have met the three criteria of being bounded, conscious affiliation to a common purpose, and self-referencing. The members define their identity collectively rather than being constructed based on decisions rules employed by the analyst. Thus, each class of network – structural, systems, and purpose has a different profile that can be described and verified in terms of the unit of theory, sampling, entitativity, and requisite characteristics.

Who Is an Analyst?

In applying this taxonomy, we make repeated reference to a mysterious being we refer to as **the analyst.** By analyst, we are referring to the person who perceives that a network exists and determines the actors and relevant ties that are its component parts. In many cases, this person will be a scholar attempting to theorize about, or study, a network. However, an analyst could also be a policy maker examining the role of networks in accomplishing policy aims. It could also be a local government official seeking to understand how to better leverage networks to improve public welfare. It could also be a grants manager at a foundation trying to decide which proposals to fund that might achieve collective impact.

Unit of Theory: The unit of theory is the most important criterion in applying this taxonomy. The unit of theory is concerned with the intent of the analyst observing a phenomenon they are conceiving of as a network. In other words, what is it the analyst wants to make statements about? If the intent of the analyst is purely to make theoretical, empirical, or practical statements about an actor or a sample of actors based on the nature of their ties to other actors and does not presume this selection of actors collectively represent some higher-order entity, this is an egocentric, structural-oriented network. If the intent of the analyst is to make statements about a sample of ties and the factors that explain change in ties over time such as understanding patterns of homophily, this is a structural-oriented dyadic network. However, if the analyst is interested in actors and/or ties in order to make statements about the micro-dynamics that drive behavior and outcomes of larger systems or a self-actualized group – the level of theory move up to either a system-oriented or purpose-oriented network. Further, care should be exercised to not confuse purpose-oriented networks with system-oriented networks as the unit of theory as they are not interchangeable. There can be multiple purpose-oriented networks operating within a given system-oriented network (see Table 1). Further, while purpose-oriented networks are often comprised of representatives from a given system of interest, the extent to which a purpose-oriented network is representative of a larger system should be approached as a diagnostic question rather than a taken-for-granted assumption.

Populating the Network: By populating the network, we refer to how the analyst decides who or what gets considered as belonging to the network and, by extension, who or what is *not* considered part of the network. While all classes of networks are comprised of actors and their relations to one another, it is important to recognize that actors can be viewed at multiple levels of analysis and this is true across all classes. In other words, actors can be individuals, institutions, or even purpose-oriented networks nested within a broader structural- or system-oriented network (see Lubell et al., 2011; Nowell et al., 2018). Defining network boundaries is an absolutely critical step for the analyst since describing networks as entities requires the delineation of the network from that which is not the network. This requires an articulation of the boundaries of the network and an acknowledgment if those boundaries are arbitrary in terms of being driven by sampling logic as opposed to reflecting a theoretical entity of interest. For example, if actors are relevant because they are connected in some theoretically important way to one or more focal actors of interest, it is a structural-oriented network. The sample size for an ego-centric network is the number of focal actors. The sample size for a dyadic network study is generally the number of ties captured; however, the boundary is arbitrary. If actors are relevant to the network because they are relevant to some system of interest, it is a system-oriented network. However, because the focus is on making descriptive or predictive statements about a system, the focus is usually on a single system. While it is possible to look at multiple system-oriented networks comparatively, it is unusual due to the feasibility constraints of measuring multiple system-oriented networks simultaneously. In a purpose-oriented network, relevant actors are defined by the network itself as a result of its bounded nature. The unit of analysis in describing a purpose-oriented network is the network. Where there are a growing number of comparative studies consisting of samples of numerous purpose-oriented networks (e.g., Nowell et al., 2018; Varda, 2020; Nowell & Albrecht, 2021), single case or small *n* comparative studies are most common (Isett et al., 2011).

Entitativity: Structurally oriented networks are delineated from the other two classes of networks on the basis of their lack of entitativity, or the presumption that actors collectively represent some higher-order system or group. In Section 3, we spoke about the nodes and edges tradition that coevolved with the development of tools like block modeling in social network analysis. Those new to the study of networks often confuse social network analysis with the study of networks as sociological entity. Social network analysis can be used to gain insight into any class of networks – what delineates the network class is the unit of theory. For example, if one is using network data to characterize the level of trust among the membership of an entity that is self-referencing and has a bounded membership that consciously affiliates around a shared purpose, then the entity being referred to as "a network" is a purpose-oriented network. Alternatively, if one is using network data to characterize referral relationships among agencies and organizations serving homeless populations within a given city in order to understand how network structure relates to community-level outcomes related to re-housing, the entity being referred to as "a network" is a system-oriented network. However, because they are nothing more than representations of social structure, structural-oriented networks are the only class of networks for which social network data are fundamental to the class. Social network data are useful in understanding other classes of network, but they are not essential. For the other classes of networks, there are multiple approaches and styles of inquiry, such as members' surveys, archival analysis, observation, and qualitative case studies, that can be used to gain insight into the governance, functioning, and performance of the network without any attention to network structure.

Requisite Characteristics: Purpose-oriented networks are a unique class of network in that they are self-actualized as entities, defined by three key characteristics: they are bounded, self-referencing, and members consciously affiliate to the network around a common purpose. These conditions are requisite and definitional to a purpose-oriented network.

Table 6 How do I know if my study/theory is a . . . .

Network Class	Unit of Theory	Population	Sample Size	Entitativity	Bounded, Self-Reference, Intentional
	"I want to make theoretical/ empirical statements about . . ."	"Actors are included in my network because . . ."	"The sample size for my study is . . ."	"This collection of actors are presumed to represent a higher order system or group . . ."	"Members of my network consciously affiliate themselves to a network entity that has given itself a name"
Structural-oriented network(s): Ego-centric	Actor(s)	They are connected in some theoretically important way to one or more focal actors of interest	# of actors	False	n/a
Structural-oriented network(s): Dyadic	Tie(s)	They are connected in some theoretically important way to one or more focal actors of interest	# of ties	False	n/a
System-oriented network(s)	System(s)	I have deemed them to play a nontrivial role in my system of interest	# of systems	True	False
Purpose-oriented network(s)	Group(s)	A group that I am interested in studying deems them to be part of the group	# of groups	True	True

Empirical Validation of the Taxonomic Class

When studying or theorizing about a network as an entity, clear articulation of the taxonomic class is vital (see Table 6 for summary). In the following section, we offer core criteria and associated indicators for validating the taxonomic class of a network entity. Each of the three classes of networks has different empirical issues that are important for an analyst to consider.

Structural-Oriented Networks: Analysts of structural-oriented networks view the world from a relational perspective (Moreno, 1934) with a focus on actors, their ties to other actors, and the consequences of those ties for either the actors or the evolution of the ties. While this may be true of analysts of system- or purpose-oriented networks as well, analysts of system- and purpose-oriented networks are interested in these dynamics in terms of their consequences for the network as an entity (purpose-oriented) or a system of interest like national defense or health care (system-oriented). Structural-oriented networks either are bounded to a focal actor (ego-centric) or are arbitrarily bounded by the analyst (dyadic) and do not represent a higher-order entity. Table 7 summarizes diagnostic questions pertinent to identifying this class of networks.

Table 7 Structural-oriented networks: Empirical validation of the taxonomic class

Characteristic	Indicators[a]
Ego-centric The network(s) of interest are the property or characteristic of an individual actor(s)	Are actors the primary unit of theory? Are actors part of the network because they are connected to a focal actor? Does the network fail to make sense as an entity if you remove the focal actor?
Dyadic The collection of actors associated with the network does not represent a higher-order entity	Are ties the primary unit of theory? Are actors included in the network purely because of identified relations to other actors? Is the boundary of the network as an entity arbitrary and/or inconsequential?

[a] Affirmative assessment suggests structural-oriented class membership.

Generalizability: A central empirical concern with structural-oriented networks is the question of generalizability. Investigations into structural-oriented networks are investigations into the consequences of relational structure for the components of networks. A central empirical question in this class of networks is whether the findings associated with the study of ego networks or ties will generalize outside of the sample. Driven by representative sampling, questions such as who are the actors, what are the ties, what is the context in which these actors are creating ties, and do the patterns that are observed in this context generalize to other actors and contexts are critical (Watts, 2004).

System-Oriented Networks: System-oriented networks are defined by an analyst based on the argument that system-level outcomes of concern are a product of the actions and interactions of an array of actors. These actors must be theorized to have some level of interconnection; however, it is possible, if not common, for certain actors or groups of actors to be disconnected from others in the network (Nowell et al., 2018). As discussed in Section 4, the central empirical concern for system-oriented networks is how the analyst is conceptualizing the system and the network of actors relevant to understanding that system. This requires a series of decision rules and associated methodology employed by the analyst to place boundaries around how they are identifying the actors that are relevant to that system. This is an interpretive process, and these decision rules have considerable consequences for defining what is knowable about a given system-oriented network. Table 8 outlines diagnostic questions for identifying networks of this class.

Table 8 System-oriented networks: Empirical validation of the taxonomic class

Characteristic	Indicators[a]
There is reason to suspect pertinent system-level outcomes of interest are the product of network actions/ interactions	Are multiple (>2) actors engaged in, contributing to, and/or undermining goal attainment of other actors in a common problem space? Are observed outcomes of interest influenced by actions and interactions among a collection (>2) of interdependent actors?
Analyst imposed decision rules are required to determine network membership and distinguish members from nonmembers	Does the analyst need to construct the network based on decision rules defined by the analyst?

Table 8 (cont.)

Characteristic	Indicators[a]
	Is it possible for different members of the network to perceive network membership differently from each other and/or from the analyst?
The network, as it has been defined by the analyst, is not self-actualized	Is it possible for network members to perceive the network and its members as an entity either not at all, inconsistently, or in vague or abstract terms?
	Would it be highly problematic for a member of the network, regardless of how central, to assert that they speak on behalf of the network as an entity?
Lack of conscious affiliation around a shared purpose	Is it possible for members to be part of the network but not know it?
	Can network members be part of the network by happenstance as a result of who they are, what they do, and/or their ego-centric relations, as opposed to intentional affiliation?

[a] Affirmative assessment suggests system-oriented class membership.

Representativeness of Networks: As discussed in Section 4, a key empirical concern with system-oriented networks relates to how much information the analyst can gather about the focal network associated with the system of interest. System-oriented networks tend to be complex and can involve a sprawling array of potentially relevant actors. It is often difficult, if not impossible, to fully represent the network of actors associated with a complex system, and the totality of their connections with each other. However, omission of key actors can fundamentally alter the "network" one perceives. As such, **analysts of system-oriented networks must first give care to describe the population of the network of interest including the decision rules used to bound this system and identify relevant actors. It is also imperative that missing data about this population of relevant actors, and the associated limitations therein, be carefully considered in making descriptive statements about a system-oriented network.** Unfortunately, unclear boundary criteria and low response rates (<50%) of the identified network are not uncommon in studies of system-oriented networks. This can lead to questionable conclusions being drawn about the system of interest, particularly in cases in which ties are not distributed equally and system-level outcomes may be strongly influenced by central actors who are not represented in the data.

Purpose-Oriented Networks Purpose-oriented networks have self-actualized as an entity. It is the role of the analyst to evaluate a network of interest to establish that the network meets the three criteria of self-actualization (see Table 9).

Table 9 Purpose-oriented networks: Empirical validation of the taxonomic class

Characteristic	Indicators[a]
Evidence exists that this network is self-referencing and has a collective identity	Has the network given itself a name? Has the network created products or artifacts such as a logo, website, or written documents that references itself as an entity? Does the network delegate individuals to represent the group, as an entity, in exchanges with external actors (e.g., there is a coordinator, chairperson, or network administrative organization authorized to speak on behalf of the network)?
Evidence exists that this network has bounded membership such that members are able to distinguish members from nonmembers	Is there a membership list that identifies who is and is not a member? Is there a recognized mechanism by which a nonmember might gain membership or a member lose membership? Do members self-identify as members? Can members collectively identify other members and distinguish them from non-members with a high degree of reliability?
Evidence exists there is a collective purpose for which members are consciously affiliating	Does the network have a statement of mission or purpose? Is there an origin story that describes why this network was convened and what precipitated its creation?

[a] Affirmative assessment suggests purpose-oriented class membership.

As discussed in Section 5, purpose-oriented networks are sometimes difficult to distinguish from system-oriented networks. This is particularly true in situations where the system of interest is highly institutionalized such that there is a common understanding of key actors that is broadly understood. For example, systems such as welfare systems, disaster response systems, and mental health systems can have some attributes akin to purpose-oriented networks. Actors within these systems have enduring relationships with one another, they often recognize one another as key stakeholders to the system and are in turn, recognized by outsiders. The system itself has an institutionalized purpose that is well understood among all stakeholders as well by citizens and politicians. However, purpose-oriented networks have unique, empirically verifiable characteristics that extend beyond heavily institutionalized system-oriented networks. It is for this reason that the characteristics of a purpose-oriented network are empirically verified by the analyst. Purpose-oriented networks can be time- and resource-limited. Once a purpose-oriented network is an entity it tends to get more cohesive as long as the resources it is dependent upon continue to flow.

Conclusion

Networks are powerful. They shape, enable, and constrain action at all levels of society. They are the social fabric that ties us together. It is no wonder that networks have captured the attention of such a diverse array of disciplines and domains of scholarship and practice over such a long period of time. Structural-oriented networks illuminate the micro-dynamics and consequences of different patterns of connectivity, focusing on the implications of these connections for actors and the evolution of network structures. System-oriented networks allow us to understand complex system behavior as a consequence of the actions and interactions of actors who control key elements and processes within a system of interest. Purpose-oriented networks highlight the power and opportunity that can come from intentional organizing as well as the challenges and requisite conditions and capacities associated with organizing and governing diverse interests.

It is hard to imagine what the fields of public management and policy would be without knowledge of networks represented in both scholarship and practice. As illustrated by the history and breadth of scholarship reviewed in this Element, we have come a long way in our understanding of all three classes of networks: structural-, systems-, and purpose-oriented. And yet, for all the knowledge we have gained, there is much we still do not understand. We have argued that one of the barriers to continuing to advance is a lack of a stable, empirically verifiable taxonomy that can meaningfully differentiate networks of different classes while at the same time offer greater opportunity for integration of multi-disciplinary perspectives of networks within the same class. Our hope is the taxonomy presented in this Element will serve as a tool to allow the field to quicken the pace of learning both within and across classes. When we are able to compare apples to apples and avoid inadvertent comparison of apples and oranges, we all get smarter faster. We look forward to continuing the journey.

References

Abson, D. J., Fischer, J., Leventon, J. et al. (2017). Leverage points for sustainability transformation. *Ambio, 46*(1), 30–39.

Ackoff, R. L. & Emery, F. E. (1972). *On purposeful systems*. Aldine-Atherton.

Agranoff, R. (2007). *Managing within networks: Adding value to public organizations*. Georgetown University Press.

Agranoff, R., & McGuire, M. (2003). Inside the matrix: Integrating the paradigms of intergovernmental and network management. *International Journal of Public Administration, 26*(12), 1401–1422.

Aiken, M., & Hage, J. (1968). Organizational interdependence and intraorganizational structure. *American Sociological Review*, 33: 912–930.

Aldrich, H. (1976). Resource dependence and interorganizational relations. *Administration and Society, 7*(4), 419–455.

Aldrich, H., & Whetten, D. (1981). Organization sets, action sets, and networks: Making the most of simplicity. In Nystrom, P and Starbuck, W., (Eds.), *Handbook of organization design, Vol 1*. (pp. 385–408). Oxford University Press.

Alter, C., & Hage, J. (1993). *Organizations working together* (Vol. 191). Sage, Incorporated.

Ansell, C., & Gash, A. (2008). Collaborative governance in theory and practice. *Journal of Public Administration Research and Theory, 18*(4), 543–571.

Ashby, W. R. (1956). *An introduction to cybernetics*. Chapman & Hall.

Astley, W. G., & Van de Ven, A. H. (1983). Central perspectives and debates in organization theory. *Administrative Science Quarterly, 28*(2), 245–273.

Atouba, Y. C., & Shumate, M. (2015). International nonprofit collaboration: Examining the role of homophily. *Nonprofit and Voluntary Sector Quarterly, 44*(3), 587–608.

Axelrod, R. (1984). *The evolution of cooperation*. Basic.

Bailey, K. D. (1994). *Typologies and taxonomies: An introduction to classification techniques*. Sage.

Barabàsi, A., & Bonabeau, E. (2003). Scale-free networks. *Scientific American, 288*(5), 60–69.

Bensen, J. K. (1975). The interorganizational network as a political economy. *Administrative Science Quarterly*, 20, 229–249.

Berardo, R. (2014). The evolution of self-organizing communication networks in high-risk social-ecological systems. *International Journal of the Commons, 8*(1), 236–258.

Berry, F. S., Brower, R. S., Choi, S. O. et al. (2004). Three traditions of network research: What the public management research agenda can learn from other research communities. *Public Administration Review, 64*(5), 539–552.

Berthod, O., & Segato, F. (2019). Developing purpose-oriented networks: A process view. *Perspectives on Public Management and Governance, 2*(3), 203–212.

Boulding, K. E. (1956). General systems theory – The skeleton of science. *Management Science, 2*(3), 197–208.

Breiger, R. L. (1976). Social structure from multiple networks. *American Journal of Sociology, 81*(4), 730–780.

Brewer, M. B., & Silver, M. D. (2000). Group distinctiveness, social identification, and collective mobilization. *Self, Identity, and Social Movements, 13*, 153–171.

Broido, A. D., & Clauset, A. (2019). Scale-free networks are rare. *Nature Communications, 10*(1), 1–10.

Brown, K., & Keast, R. (2003). Citizen-government engagement: Community connection through networked arrangements. *Asian Journal of Public Administration, 25*(1), 107–131.

Bryson, J. M., & Crosby, B. C.
   (1992). *Leadership for the common good – Tackling public problems when no one is in charge (2nd ed)* Jossey-Bass.
   (2005). *Leaders.hip for the common good – Tackling public problems when no one is in charge.* Jossey-Bass.

Bryson, J. M., Crosby, B. C., & Stone, M. M. (2006). The design and implementation of cross-sector collaborations: Propositions from the literature. *Public Administration Review, 66*, 44–55.

Bryson, J. M., Crosby, B. C., & Stone, M. M. (2015). Designing and implementing cross-sector collaborations: Needed and challenging. *Public Administration Review, 75*(5), 647–663.

Burns, T. & Stalker, G. M. (1961). Mechanistic and organic systems of management. Reprinted (1994) In *The Management of Innovation* rev (pp. 96–125). Oxford University Press.

Burns, T., & Stalker, G. M. (1961). *The management of innovation.* Tavistock.

Burt, R. S. (1995). *Structural holes: The social structure of competition.* Harvard University Press.

Burt, R. S., Kilduff, M., & Tasselli, S. (2013). Social network analysis: Foundations and frontiers on advantage. *Annual Review of Psychology, 64*, 527–547.

Burt, R. S. (1997). The contingent value of social capital. *Administrative Science Quarterly, 42*(2), 339–365.

Burt, R. S. (2001). Structural holes versus network closure as social capital. In N. Lin, K. Cook, & R. S. Burt (Eds.), *Social capital: Theory and research*, (pp. 31–55). Taylor Francis.

Burt, R. S. (2004). Structural holes and good ideas. *American Journal of Sociology, 110*(2), 349–399.

Carboni, J. L., Saz-Carranza, A., Raab, J., & Isett, K. R. (2019). Taking dimensions of purpose-oriented networks seriously. *Perspectives on Public Management and Governance, 2*(3), 187–223.

Cater, D. (1964). *Power in Washington.* Vintage. *Change, 14*(2), 527–539.

Chapman, C. L., & Varda, D. M. (2017). Nonprofit resource contribution and mission alignment in interorganizational, cross-sector public health networks. *Nonprofit and Voluntary Sector Quarterly, 46*(5), 1052–1072.

Coleman, J. S. (1988). Social capital in the creation of human capital. *American Journal of Sociology, 94*, S95–S120.

Comfort, L. K. (2007). Crisis management in hindsight: Cognition, communication, coordination, and control. *Public Administration Review, 67*, 189–197.

Conner, D. S., King, B., Koliba, C., Kolodinsky, J., & Trubek, A. (2011). Mapping farm-to-school networks implications for research and practice. *Journal of Hunger & Environmental Nutrition, 6*(2), 133–152.

D'Andreta, D., Marabelli, M., Newell, S., Scarbrough, H., & Swan, J. (2016). Dominant cognitive frames and the innovative power of social networks. *Organization Studies, 37*(3), 293–321.

Dahl, R., & Lindblom, C. E. (1953). *Politics, economics and welfare.* Harper and Row.

Damanpour, F. (1991). Organizational innovation: A meta-analysis of effects of determinants and moderators. *Academy of Management Journal, 34*(3), 555–590.

Davidson, R. H. (1974). Policy making in the manpower subgovernment. In Michael D. Smith (Ed.), *Policies in America: Studies in policy analysis.* Random House, 82–106.

Derrida, J. (1992). *The other heading: Reflections on today's Europe.* Indiana University Press.

Drabek, T. E. (1983). Alternative patterns of decision-making in emergent disaster response networks. *International Journal of Mass Emergencies and Disasters, 1*(2), 277–305.

Dryzek, J. S. (2000). *Deliberative democracy and beyond: Liberals, critics, contestations.* Oxford University Press.

Eden, C., & Ackermann, F. (1998). *Making strategy: The journey of strategic management.* Sage.

Elmore, R. F. (1979). Backward mapping: Implementation research and policy decisions. *Political Science Quarterly, 94*(Winter), 601–616.

Emerson, K., & Nabatchi, T. (2015). *Collaborative governance regimes.* Georgetown University Press.

Emerson, K., Nabatchi, T., & Balogh, S. (2012). An integrative framework for collaborative governance. *Journal of Public Administration Research and Theory, 65*(5), 1–29.

Emery, F. E., & Trist, E. L. (1965). The causal texture of organizational environments. *Human Relations, 18*(1), 21–32.

Emery, F. E., & Trist, E. L. (1973). Task and contextual environments for new personal values. In *Towards a Social Ecology* (pp. 182–189). Springer.

Evan, W. F. (1965). Toward a theory of inter-organizational relations. *Management Science, 11* (10), B-217–B-230.

Evan, W. M. (1972). An organization-set model of interorganizational relations. In R. Chisholm (Ed.), *Interorganizational decisionmaking* (pp. 181–200). Aldine.

Faulk, L., Willems, J., McGinnis Johnson, J., & Stewart, A. J. (2016). Network connections and competitively awarded funding: The impacts of board network structures and status interlocks on nonprofit organizations' foundation grant acquisition. *Public Management Review, 18*(10), 1425–1455.

Feldman, M. S., & Sengupta, P. (2020). Enacting the logic of possibility in organizations and management. *Perspectives on Public Management and Governance, 3*(2), 95–107.

Foster-Fishman, P. G., Nowell, B., & Yang, H. (2007). Putting the system back into systems change: A framework for understanding and changing organizational and community systems. *American Journal of Community Psychology, 39*(3–4), 197–215.

Foucault, M. (1991). *The Foucault effect: Studies in governmentality.* University of Chicago Press.

Frank, K. A. (2009). Quasi-ties: Directing resources to members of a collective. *American Behavioral Scientist, 52*(12), 1613–1645.

Freeman, J. L. (1955). *The political process.* Random House.

Freeman, L. (2004). The development of social network analysis. *A Study in the Sociology of Science, 1*(687), 159–167.

Friend, J., & Hickling, A. (1987). *Planning under pressure.* Pergamon Press.

Friis, C., & Østergaard, N. J. (2017). On the system boundary choices, implications, and solutions in telecoupling land use change research. *Sustainability, 9*(6), 974.

Fritchler, A. (1969). *Smoking and politics: Policy-making and the federal bureaucracy.* Appleton-Century-Crofts.

Frumkin, P., & Reingold, D. (2004) Why programs get replicated. *Nonprofit Quarterly*, Fall: 46–59.

Galloway, A. R., & Thacker, E. (2013). *The exploit: A theory of networks* (Vol. 21). University of Minnesota Press.

Giddens, A. (1976). *New rules of sociological method*. Hutchinson.

Giddens, A. (1984). *The constitution of society*. Polity Press.

Glisson, C., & Hemmelgarn, A. (1998). The effects of organizational climate and interorganizational coordination on the quality and outcomes of children's service systems. *Child Abuse & Neglect, 22*(5), 401–421.

Granovetter, M. S. (1973). The strength of weak ties. *American Journal of Sociology, 78*(6), 1360–1380.

Gray, B. (1989). *Collaborating*. Jossey-Bass.

Gray, B., & Purdy, J. (2018). *Collaborating for our future: Multistakeholder partnerships for solving complex problems*. Oxford University Press.

Griffith, E. S. (1939). *Impasse of democracy*. Harrison-Hilton.

Hammond, D. (2002). Exploring the genealogy of systems thinking. *Systems Research and Behavioral Science, 19*(5), 429–439.

Hanf, K., & Scharpf, F. W. (Eds.) (1978). *Interorganizational policy making: Limits to coordination and central control*. Sage Modern Politics Series Vol. 1 sponsored by the European Consortium for Political Research. Sage.

Hanf, K., Hjern, B., & Porter, D. (1978). Local networks of manpower training in the federal republic of Germany and Sweden. In Hanf, Kenneth & F. W. Scharpf (Eds.), *Interorganizational policy making: Limits to coordination and central control* (pp. 303–341). Sage Modern Politics Series Vol. 1 sponsored by the European Consortium for Political Research. Sage.

Heclo, H. (1978). Issue networks and the executive establishment. In A. King (Ed.), *The new American political system* (pp. 413–422). American Enterprise Institute.

Hegele, Y. (2018). Explaining bureaucratic power in intergovernmental relations: A network approach. *Public Administration: An International Quarterly, 96*, 753–768.

Henry, A. D., Lubell, M., & McCoy, M. (2011). Belief systems and social capital as drivers of policy network structure: The case of California regional planning. *Journal of Public Administration Research and Theory, 21*(3), 419–444.

Herzog, P. S., & Yang, S. (2018). Social networks and charitable giving: Trusting, doing, asking, and alter primacy. *Nonprofit and Voluntary Sector Quarterly, 47*(2), 376–394.

Hirschman, D., & Reed, I. A. (2014). Formation stories and causality in sociology. *Sociological Theory, 32*(4), 259–282.

Hjern, B., & Porter, D. O. (1981). Implementation structures: A new unit of administrative analysis. *Organizational Studies, 2*(3), 211–227.

Hodgson, G. M. (2019). Taxonomic definitions in social science, with firms, markets and institutions as case studies. *Journal of Institutional Economics, 15*(2), 207–233.

Holme, P. (2019). Rare and everywhere: Perspectives on scale-free networks. *Nature Communications, 10*(1), 1–3.

Hugg, V. G. (2019). Public service-function types and interlocal agreement network structure: A longitudinal study of Iowa. *Urban Affairs Review, 56*(4), 1293–1315.

Human, S. E., & Provan, K. G. (2000). Legitimacy building in the evolution of small-firm multilateral networks: A comparative study of success and demise. *Administrative Science Quarterly, 45*(2), 327–365.

Huxham, C., & Vangen, S. (2013). *Managing to collaborate: The theory and practice of collaborative advantage.* Routledge University Press.

Hwang, H., & Colyvas, J. A. (2020). Ontology, levels of society, and degrees of generality: Theorizing actors as abstractions in institutional theory. *Academy of Management Review, 45*(3), 570–595.

Iborra, S. S., Saz-Carranza, A., Fernández-i-Marín, X., & Albareda, A. (2018). The governance of goal-directed networks and network tasks: An empirical analysis of European regulatory networks. *Journal of Public Administration Research and Theory, 28*(2), 270–292.

Isett, K. R., Mergel, I. A., LeRoux, K., Mischen, P. A., & Rethemeyer, R. K. (2011). Networks in public administration scholarship: Understanding where we are and where we need to go. *Journal of Public Administration Research and Theory, 21* (suppl_1), i157–i173.

Jenkins-Smith, H. C., Nohrstedt, D., Weible, C. M., & Sabatier, P. A. (2014). The advocacy coalition framework: Foundations, evolution, and ongoing research. *Theories of the Policy Process, 3*, 183–224.

Joosse, A. P., & Milward, H. B. (2017). Health policy networks. In Victor, J. N., Montgomery, A. H. & Lubell, M. *The Oxford handbook of political networks*, Oxford University Press, 627–647.

Kammerer, M., & Namhata, C. (2018). What drives the adoption of climate change mitigation policy? A dynamic network approach to policy diffusion. *Policy Sciences, 51*(4), 477–513.

Kania, J., & Kramer, M. (2011). *Collective Impact.* Stanford Social Innovation Review. https://senate.humboldt.edu/sites/default/files/senate/Chair%20Written%20Report%201-23-2018.pdf

Kaplan, A. (1964). *The conduct of inquiry.* Chandler.

Kapucu, N. (2006). Interagency communication networks during emergencies: Boundary spanners in multiagency coordination. *The American Review of Public Administration, 36*(2), 207–225.

Kapucu, N., & Garayev, V. (2016). Structure and network performance: Horizontal and vertical networks in emergency management. *Administration & Society, 48*(8), 931–961.

Kapucu, N., & Hu, Q. (2020). *Network governance: Concepts, theories, and applications*. Routledge.

Kapucu, N., Hu, Q., & Khosa, S. (2014). The state of network research in public administration. *Administration & Society, 1*, 34.

Katz, D., & Kahn, R. L. (1966). *The social psychology of organizations*. Wiley.

Keast, R. (2016). Network governance. In *Handbook on theories of governance* (edited by C. Ansell and J. Torfing), Edward Elgar.

Keast, R., Brown, K., & Mandell, M. (2007). Getting the right mix: Unpacking integration meanings and strategies. *International Public Management Journal, 10*(1), 9–33.

Keast, R., Mandell, M. P., Brown, K., & Woolcock, G. (2004). Network structures: Working differently and changing expectations. *Public Administration Review, 64*(3), 363–371.

Kenis, P. (2016). *Networks*. In C. Ansell, & J. Torfing (Eds)., *Handbook on theories of governance*. Edward Elgar.

Kickert, W. J., Klijn, E. H., & Koppenjan, J. F. (Eds.). (1997). *Managing complex networks: Strategies for the public sector*. Sage.

Kiser, L. L., & Ostrom, E. (1982). The three worlds of action: A metatheoretical synthesis of institutional approaches, In E. Ostrom (Ed.), *Strategies for political inquiry* (pp. 179–222). Sage.

Klijn, E. H. (2008). Governance and governance networks in Europe: An assessment of ten years of research on the theme. *Public Management Review, 10*(4), 505–525.

Klijn, E. H. (2020). Network management in public administration: The essence of network and collaborative governance. In *Oxford research encyclopedia of politics* (edited by W. Thompson). Oxford University Press. https://doi.org/10.1093/acrefore/978019228637.013.1418

Klijn, E. H., & Koppenjan, J. (2016). The 11 shift toward network governance. *Theory and Practice of Public Sector Reform, 27*, 158.

Klijn, E. H., & Koppenjan, J. F. (2000). Public management and policy networks: Foundations of a network approach to governance. *Public Management an International Journal of Research and Theory, 2*(2), 135–158.

Koliba, C. J., Meek, J. W., Zia, A., & Mills, R. W. (2018). *Governance networks in public administration and public policy*. Routledge.

Koliba, C. J., Mills, R. M., & Zia, A. (2011). Accountability in governance networks: An assessment of public, private, and nonprofit emergency management practices following Hurricane Katrina. *Public Administration Review, 71*(2), 210–220.

Kramer, R. M., Brewer, M. B., & Hanna, B. A. (1996). Collective trust and collective action. In R. M. Kramer & T. R. Tyler (Eds.), *Trust in organizations: Frontiers of theory and research* (pp. 357–389). Sage.

Laumann, E. O., & Knoke, D. (1987). *The organizational state: Social choice in national policy domains*. University of Wisconsin Press.

Laumann, E. O., Galaskiewicz, J., & Marsden, P. V. (1978). Community structure as interorganizational linkages. *Annual Review of Sociology, 4*, 455–484.

Laumann, E. O., Marsden, P. V., & Prensky, D. (1983). The boundary specification problem in network analysis. In R. S. Burt & M. J. Minor (Eds.), *Applied network analysis: A methodological introduction* (pp. 18–34). Sage.

Laumann, E. O., Marsden, P. V., & Prensky, D. (1989). The boundary specification problem in network analysis. *Research Methods in Social Network Analysis, 61*, 87.

Lawrence, P. R., & Lorsch, J. W. (1967). Differentiation and integration in complex organizations. *Administrative Science Quarterly, 12*,1–47.

Lawrence, P., & Lorsch, J. (1967). *Organization and environment*. Harvard University Press.

Lecy, J. D., Mergel, I. A., & Schmitz, H. P. (2014). Networks in public administration: Current scholarship in review. *Public Management Review, 16*(5), 643–665.

Lemaire, R. H. (2020). What is our purpose here? Network relationships and goal congruence in a goal-directed network. *The American Review of Public Administration, 50*(2), 176–192.

Lemaire, R. H., & Provan, K. G. (2012). *Managing collaborative effort: A dyadic analysis of a public goal-directed network*. Working Paper. www .researchgate.net/profile/Keith_Provan/publication/228509005_Managing_ Collaborative_Effort_A_Dyadic_Analysis_of_a_Public_Goaldirected_Net work/links/5626849f08ae4d9e5c4d342d.pdf.

Lemaire, R. H., Mannak, R. S., Ospina, S. M., & Groenleer, M. (2019). Striving for state of the art with paradigm interplay and meta-synthesis: Purpose-oriented network research challenges and good research practices as a way forward. *Perspectives on Public Management and Governance, 2*(3), 175–208.

Levin, S., & White, P. E. (1961). Exchange as a conceptual framework for the study of interorganizational relationships. *Administrative Science Quarterly, 5*(4), 583–601.

Litwak, E., & Hylton, L. F. (1962). Interorganizational analysis: A hypothesis on co-ordinating agencies. *Administrative Science Quarterly, 6,* 395–420.

Long, N. (1958). The local community as an ecology of games. *American Journal of Sociology, 64*(3), 251–261.

Lubell, M. (2013). Governing institutional complexity: The ecology of games framework. *Policy Studies Journal, 41*(3), 537–559.

Lubell, M. N., Robins, G., & Wang, P. (2011). *Policy coordination in an ecology of water management games.* Paper 22. http://opensiuc.lib.siu.edu /pnconfs_2011/22.

Lubell, M., & Fulton, A. (2008). Local policy networks and agricultural watershed management. *Journal of Public Administration Research and Theory, 18*(4), 673–696.

Maass, A. (1951). *Muddy waters: The Army engineers and the nation's rivers.* Harvard University Press.

Maslow, A. H. (1967). A theory of metamotivation: The biological rooting of the value-life. *Journal of Humanistic Psychology, 7*(2), 93–127.

Mayer, R. R. (1972). Social system models for planners. *Journal of the American Institute of Planners, 38*(3): 130–139.

McAllister, R. R. J., McCrea, R., & Lubell, M. N. (2014). Policy networks, stakeholder interactions and climate adaptation in the region of South East Queensland, Australia. *Regional Environmental Change, 14*(2), 527–539.

Meier, K. J., & O'Toole Jr, L. J. (2001). Managerial strategies and behavior in networks: A model with evidence from US public education. *Journal of Public Administration Research and Theory, 11*(3), 271–294.

Merriam-Webster. (n.d.). Actualize. In *Merriam-Webster.com dictionary.* Retrieved April 27, 2021, www.merriam-webster.com/dictionary/actualize.

Mills, C. W. (1959). *The power elite.* Oxford University Press.

Milward, H. B. (1982). Interorganizational policy systems and research on public organizations. *Administration and Society, 13*(4), 457–478.

Milward, H. B., & Provan, K. G. (1998). Measuring network structure. *Public Administration, 76*(2), 387–407.

Milward, H. B., & Provan, K. G. (2000). Governing the hollow state. *Journal of Public Administration Research and Theory, 10*(2), 359–380.

Milward, H. B., & Wamsley, G. L. (1985). Policy subsystems, networks and the tools of public policy. In K. F. Hanf & T. A. J. Toonen (Eds.), *Policy implementation in federal and unitary systems* (pp. 105–130). Martinus Nijhoff Publishers.

Milward, H. B. & Provan, K. G. (2006). *A Manager's Guide to Choosing and Using Collaborative Networks.* Networks and Partnerships Series, IBM Center for the Business of Government.

Milward, H. B., Cooper, K. R., & Shumate, M. (2016) Who says a common agenda is necessary for Collective Impact? Summer, 41–43. www.npqmag.org.

Mingers, J., & White, L. (2010). A review of the recent contribution of systems thinking to operational research and management science. *European Journal of Operational Research, 207*(3), 1147–1161.

Mitchell, J. C. (Ed.). (1969). *Social networks in urban situations: Analyses of personal relationships in Central African towns*. Manchester University Press.

Moreno, J. L. (1934). *Who shall survive?*. Nervous and Mental Disease.

Moreno, J. L. (1934). *Who shall survive?: A new approach to the problem of human interrelations*. Nervous and Mental Disease.

Moynihan, D. P. (2009). The network governance of crisis response. *Journal of Public Administration Research and Theory, 19*(4), 895–915.

Nisar, M. A., & Maroulis, S. (2017). Foundations of relating: Theory and evidence on the formation of street-level bureaucrats' workplace networks. *Public Administration Review, 77*(6), 829–839.

Nohrstedt, D., & Bodin, Ö. (2019). Collective action problem characteristics and partner uncertainty as drivers of social tie formation in collaborative networks: Social tie formation in collaborative networks. *Policy Studies Journal, 48*(4), 1082–1108.

Nolte, I. M., & Boenigk, S. (2011). Public-nonprofit partnership performance in a disaster context: The case of Haiti. *Public Administration, 89*(4), 1385–1402.

North, D. C. (1990). *Institutions, institutional change and economic performance*. Cambridge University Press.

Nowell, B., Bodkin, C. P., & Bayoumi, D. (2017). Redundancy as a strategy in disaster response systems: A pathway to resilience or a recipe for disaster? *Journal of Contingencies and Crisis Management, 25*(3), 123–135.

Nowell, B. L., & Kenis, P. (2019). Purpose-oriented networks: The architecture of complexity. *Perspectives on Public Management and Governance, 2*(3), 169–173.

Nowell, B., & Steelman, T. (2013). 12 The role of responder networks in promoting community resilience. *Disaster resiliency: Interdisciplinary perspectives, 4*, 232.

(2019). Beyond ICS: How should we govern complex disasters in the United States? *Journal of Homeland Security and Emergency Management, 16* (2), 1–5.

Nowell, B., Steelman, T., Velez, A. L. K., & Yang, Z. (2018). The structure of effective governance of disaster response networks: Insights from the field. *The American Review of Public Administration, 48*(7), 699–715.

Nowell, B. L., Velez, A. L. K., Hano, M. C. et al. (2018). Studying networks in complex problem domains: Advancing methods in boundary specification. *Perspectives on Public Management and Governance, 1*(4), 273–282.

Ofem, B., Arya, B., & Borgatti, S. P. (2018). The drivers of collaborative success between rural economic development organizations. *Nonprofit and Voluntary Sector Quarterly, 47*(6), 1113–1134.

Opsahl, T., Vernet, A., Alnuaimi, T., & George, G. (2017). Revisiting the small-world phenomenon: Efficiency variation and classification of small-world networks. *Organizational Research Methods, 20*(1), 149–173.

Ostrom, E. (2011). Background on the institutional analysis and development framework. *Policy Studies Journal, 39*(1), 7–27.

Ostrom, E., Parks, R. B., & Whitaker, G. P. (1974). Defining and measuring structural variations in interorganizational arrangements. *Publius, 4*(4), 87–108.

O'Toole Jr., L. J., & Meier, K. J. (2003). Plus ça change: Public management, personnel stability, and organizational performance. *Journal of Public Administration Research and Theory, 13*, 43–64.

Ouchi, W. G. (1991). Markets, bureaucracies and clans. In G. Thompson, J. Frances, R. Levacic, & J. Mitchell (Eds.), *Markets, hierarchies and networks. The coordination of social life* (pp. 246–255). Sage.

Pachucki, M. C., & Lewis, K. (2017). Networks at Harvard University Sociology. In R. Alhaji & J. Rokne (Eds.), *Encyclopedia of social network analysis and mining.* https://doi.org/10.1007/978-1-4614-7163-9_73–1.

Park, H. H., & Rethemeyer, R. K. (2014). The politics of connections: Assessing the determinants of social structure in policy networks. *Journal of Public Administration Research and Theory, 24*(2), 349–379.

Pfeffer, J., & Salancik, G. R. (1978). *The external control of organizations: A resource dependence perspective.* Harper & Row.

Polanyi, M. (1951). *The logic of liberty.* University of Chicago Press.

Pollack Porter, K. M., Rutkow, L., & McGinty, E. E. (2018). The importance of policy change for addressing public health problems. *Public Health Reports, 133*(1_suppl), 9S-14S.

Powell, R. (1991). Absolute and relative gains in international relations theory. *The American Political Science Review, 85*, 1303–1320.

Pressman, J. L., & Wildavsky A. B. (1973). *Implementation: How great expectations in Washington are dashed in Oakland, or why it's amazing that federal programs work at all.* University of California Press.

Provan, K. G., Fish, A., & Sydow, J. (2007). Interorganizational networks at the network level: A review of the empirical literature on whole networks. *Journal of Management, 33*(3), 479–516.

Provan, K. G., & Kenis, P. (2008). Modes of network governance: Structure, management, and effectiveness. *Journal of Public Administration Research and Theory*, *18*(2), 229–252.

Provan, K. G., & Milward, H. B. (1995). A preliminary theory of interorganizational network effectiveness: A comparative study of four community mental health systems. *Administrative Science Quarterly*, 40, 1–33.

Raab, J., & Kenis, P. (2009). Heading toward a society of networks: Empirical developments and theoretical challenges. *Journal of Management Inquiry*, *18*(3), 198–210.

Raab, J., Mannak, R. S., & Cambré, B. (2015). Combining structure, governance, and context: A configurational approach to network effectiveness. *Journal of Public Administration Research and Theory*, *25*(2), 479–511.

Redford, E. S. (1960). A case analysis of Congressional activity: Civil aviation, 1957–1958. *Journal of Politics*, *22*(2), 228–258.

Rethemeyer, R. K., & Hatmaker, D. M. (2008). Network management reconsidered: An inquiry into management of network structures in public sector service provision. *Journal of Public Administration Research and Theory*, *18*(4), 617–646.

Rhodes, R. A. W. (2008). Policy network analysis. In R. E. Goodin, M. Moran, & M. Rein (Eds.), *The oxford handbook of public policy* (pp. 425–447). Oxford University Press.

Rhodes, M. L., & Murray, J. (2007). Collaborative decision making in urban regeneration: A complex adaptive systems perspective. *International Public Management Journal*, *10*(1), 79–101.

Richman, B. D. (2006). How community institutions create economic advantage: Jewish diamond merchants in New York. *Law & Social Inquiry*, *31*(2), 383–420.

Rittel, H. W., & Webber, M. M. (1973). Dilemmas in a general theory of planning. *Policy Sciences*, *4*(2), 155–169.

Rogers, E. M. (1962). *Diffusion of innovations*. Free Press of Glencoe.

Sabatier, P. A. (1987). Knowledge, policy-oriented learning, and policy change: An advocacy coalition framework. *Knowledge*, *8*(4), 649–692.

Sabatier, P., & Mazmanian, D. (1979). The conditions of effective implementation: A guide to accomplishing policy objectives. *Policy Analysis*, *5*(4), 481–504.

Saz-Carranza, A. (2012). *Uniting diverse organizations: Managing goal-oriented advocacy networks*. Routledge.

Saz-Carranza, A., & Ospina, S. M. (2011). The behavioral dimension of governing interorganizational goal-directed networks – Managing the unity-diversity tension. *Journal of Public Administration Research and Theory*, *21*(2), 327–365.

Scharpf, F. W. (1978). Comparative policy studies: Cases in search of systematic theory. *European Journal of Political Research, 6*(1), 117–125.

Scharpf, F. W. (1978). Interorganizational policy studies: Issues, concepts, and perspectives. In Hanf, Kenneth and Fritz W. Scharpf (Eds.), *Interorganizational policy making: Limits to coordination and central control* (pp. 345–370). Sage Modern Politics Series Vol. 1 sponsored by the European Consortium for Political Research. Sage.

Scharpf, F. W. (1997). Introduction: the problem-solving capacity of multi-level governance. *Journal of European Public Policy, 4*(4), 520–538.

Schmitter, P. C. (1974). Still the century of corporatism?. *The Review of Politics, 36*(1), 85–131.

Shumate, M., & Cooper, K. R. (2016). *Collective impact: What we really know.* Network for Nonprofit and Social Impact, Northwestern University. https://nnsi.soc.northwestern.edu/wp-content/uploads/2016/05/Collective-impact-Report-Final.pdf

Siciliano, M. D. (2016). Ignoring the experts: Networks and organizational learning in the public sector. *Journal of Public Administration Research and Theory, 27*(1), 104–119.

Siciliano, M. D., Wang, W., & Medina, A. (2021). Mechanisms of network formation in the public sector: A systematic review of the literature. *Perspectives on Public Management and Governance, 4*(1), 63–81.

Simo, G., & Bies, A. L. (2007). The role of nonprofits in disaster response: An expanded model of cross-sector collaboration. *Public administration review, 67*, 125–142.

Simon, H. A. (1946). The proverbs of administration. *Public Administration Review, 6*(1), 53–67.

Simon, H. A. (1962). The architecture of complexity. *American Philosophical Society, 106*(6), 467–482.

Smith, K. B. (2002). Typologies, taxonomies, and the benefits of policy classification. *Policy Studies Journal, 30*(3), 379–395.

Sørensen, E., & Torfing, J. (2005). The democratic anchorage of governance networks. *Scandinavian Political Studies, 28*(3), 195–218.

Spencer, H. (1897). *Principles of sociology* (Vol. 6). D. Appleton and Company.

Tasselli, S. (2015). Social networks and inter-professional knowledge transfer: The case of healthcare professionals. *Organization Studies, 36*(7), 841–872.

Thompson, J. D. (1967). *Organizations in action.* McGraw Hill.

Torfing, J. (2012). Governance networks. *The Oxford Handbook of Governance,* edited by D. Levi-Faur: Retrieved from //www.oxfordhandbooks.com/, Oxford Handbooks Online (2012) 10.1093/oxfordhb/9780199560530.001.0001/oxfordhb-9780199560530-e-7. Oxford University Press.

Trist, E. (1983). Referent organizations and the development of inter-organizational domains. *Human Relations, 36*(3), 269–284.

Tsoukas, H. (2016). Don't simplify, complexify: From disjunctive to conjunctive theorizing in organization and management studies. *Journal of Management Studies, 54*(2), 132–153.

Tulin, M., Volker, B., & Lancee, B. (2019). The same place but different: How neighborhood context differentially affects homogeneity in networks of different social groups. *Journal of Urban Affairs, 43*(1), 57–76.

Turner, J. C. (2010). Social categorization and the self-concept: A social cognitive theory of group behavior. In T. Postmes & N. R. Branscombe (Eds.), *Key readings in social psychology. Rediscovering social identity* (pp. 243–272). Psychology Press.

Vantaggiato, F. P. (2018). The drivers of regulatory networking: policy learning between homophily and convergence. *Journal of Public Policy, 39*(3), 443–464.

Vantaggiato, F., & Lubell, M. (2020, September 24). *The Benefits of Specialization in Collaborative Governance Forums.* Paper presented for the ESADE/Tilburg Network Webinar Series.

Varda, D. M., & Sprong, S. (2020). Evaluating networks using PARTNER: A social network data tracking and learning tool. *New Directions for Evaluation, 2020*(165), 67–89.

Von Bertalanffy, L. (1951). "General System Theory – A new approach to unity of science" (Symposium). *Human Biology, 23*(4), 303–361.

Warren, R. L. (1967). The interorganizational field as a focus for investigation. *Administrative Science Quarterly,* 12, 396–419.

Wasserman, S., & Faust, K. (1994). *Social network analysis: Methods and applications.* Cambridge University Press.

Watts, D. J. (2004). The "new" science of networks. *Annual Review of Sociology, 30,* 243–270.

Weber, M. (1949). *Max Weber on the methodology of the social sciences.* Free Press.

Weick, K. E. (1969). *The social psychology of organizing.* Addison-Wesley.

Weick, K. E. (1989). Organized improvisation: 20 years of organizing. *Communication Studies, 40*(4), 241–248.

Wenger, E. (1998). *Communities of practice: Learning, meaning and identity.* Cambridge University Press.

White, H. C. (1970). *Chains of opportunity: System models of mobility in organizations.* Harvard University Press.

White, H. C., Boorman, S. A., & Breiger, R. L. (1976). Social structure from multiple networks. I. Blockmodels of roles and positions. *American Journal of Sociology, 81*(4), 730–780.

Wikileaks (2011). Global Futures Forum, https://wikileaks.org/gifiles/attach/7/7023_What%20Is%20GFF%202011.pdf

Wildavsky, A. (1979). *Speaking truth to power: The art and craft of policy analysis.* Little Brown and Company.

Williamson, O. E. (1975). *Markets and hierarchies: Analysis and antitrust implications.* The Free Press.

Xu, W., & Saxton, G. D. (2019). Does stakeholder engagement pay off on social media? A social capital perspective. *Nonprofit and Voluntary Sector Quarterly, 48*(1), 28–49.

Zafonte, M., & Sabatier, P. (1998). Shared beliefs and imposed interdependencies as determinants of ally networks in overlapping subsystems. *Journal of Theoretical Politics, 10*(4), 473–505.

Zald, M. N. (1970). *Organizational change: The political economy of the YMCA.* University of Chicago Press.

Zarghami, M., & Akbariyeh, S. (2012). System dynamics modeling for complex urban water systems: Application to the city of Tabriz, Iran. *Resources, Conservation and Recycling, 60*, 99–106.

Acknowledgments

This manuscript benefited significantly from the thoughtful insights and feedback of our colleagues in the world of networks and collaboration. We want to thank John Bryson, Patrick Kenis, Christopher Koliba, and Michael Siciliano for their early review of the manuscript as well as our blind peer reviewer. We would like to thank Kirk Emerson, John Bryson, Chris Huxham, Siv Vangen, Mark Lubell, Naim Kapucu, and Chris Weible for their help with the origins of research on networks and collaboration. Thanks to Joaquin Herranz for suggesting the title for Section 6. We would also like to acknowledge and express our deep appreciation for the amazing community of public/nonprofit management and policy network scholars who have inspired much of the thinking that resulted in this manuscript. Special thanks to Jörg Raab and Angel Saz-Carranza as well as to Örjan Bodin and Daniel Nohrstedt for their leadership in helping to organize this community. Thanks to our editors, Andy Whitford and Rob Christianson. Finally, heartfelt thanks to Shannon McGovern for her editorial assistance.

Cambridge Elements ≡

Public and Nonprofit Administration

Andrew Whitford

University of Georgia

Andrew Whitford is Alexander M. Crenshaw Professor of Public Policy in the School of Public and International Affairs at the University of Georgia. His research centers on strategy and innovation in public policy and organization studies.

Robert Christensen

Brigham Young University

Robert Christensen is Professor and George Romney Research Fellow in the Marriott School at Brigham Young University. His research focuses on prosocial and antisocial behaviors and attitudes in public and nonprofit organizations.

About the Series

The foundation of this series are cutting-edge contributions on emerging topics and definitive reviews of keystone topics in public and nonprofit administration, especially those that lack longer treatment in textbook or other formats. Among keystone topics of interest for scholars and practitioners of public and nonprofit administration, it covers public management, public budgeting and finance, nonprofit studies, and the interstitial space between the public and nonprofit sectors, along with theoretical and methodological contributions, including quantitative, qualitative and mixed-methods pieces.

The Public Management Research Association

The Public Management Research Association improves public governance by advancing research on public organizations, strengthening links among interdisciplinary scholars, and furthering professional and academic opportunities in public management.

Cambridge Elements ☰

Public and Nonprofit Administration

Printed in the United States
by Baker & Taylor Publisher Services